LEFT FOR DEAD
K.A. PAUL OF INDIA

With a Foreword by
Coach Bill McCartney

LEFT FOR DEAD
K.A. PAUL OF INDIA

Published By Encourager Media
10950 Old Katy Road
Houston, Texas 77043
1-800-964-1018

Copyright, K.A. Paul, 1997

Scripture quotes from New American Standard Standard Version unless otherwise noted, copyright, The Lockman Foundation, La Habra, California.

TABLE OF CONTENTS

Foreword–Coach Bill McCartney
From His Excellency, the Mayor of Kurnool, India

1–Left For Dead — *Page 1*
2–Venkata Rao Becomes 'Barnabas' — *Page 6*
3–A Christian Home In India — *Page 18*
4–Journey To Hell — *Page 30*
5–Call To Orissa — *Page 42*
6–The First of the 'Unreached Millions' — *Page 49*
7–A Cow-Shed Resting Place — *Page 55*
8–Conversion Leads To Torture — *Page 63*
9–Marriage — *Page 70*
10–Living At The Edge — *Page 81*
11–Power In Ministry — *Page 91*
12–The Ministry Of Healing — *Page 99*
13–Kidnapped In Calcutta — *Page 107*
14–Back To Life — *Page 123*

FOREWORD

By Coach Bill McCartney

> I have a passion burning in my heart. My passion is to see this world won for Jesus.

I have a passion burning in my heart. My passion is to see this world won for Jesus.

In February, 1996, I stood for the first time in a region of the world which has become known as the 10-40 Window, the area between the 10th latitude North and the 40th latitude South. From Spain to Japan, 4.1 billion live in this area. Of these 4.1 billion people, nearly 3 billion have never heard the Name of Jesus. That fact is beyond my comprehension!

Standing in open air crusades in India, I saw with my own eyes thousands coming to Christ. I had never seen anything like this! Tens of thousands have responded to the call to leave their homes and jobs to be trained and sent out as evangelists to the people in the 10-40 Window. These people knew that this call was to go into regions where there has been no witness of Christ for over two millennia!

They knew they might be beaten and ridiculed.

Some of them would even be killed, and yet they still came.

The only hindrance to their going is the need for training, transportation and support. Even now I am deeply moved by the memory of these radical lovers of Jesus whose hunger to follow Christ's command is so authentic.

I am committed to doing everything I can to lend my personal energies to the releasing of these evangelists to go to the billions in China, Bhutan, Bangladesh, India, Pakistan, Thailand, Afghanistan and Nepal and all the 66 countries in the 10-40 Window.

Let me speak to you from my heart. I have joined hands with Gospel to the Unreached Millions to reach the unreached world to finish the task. Dr. K.A. Paul, the Founder of this ministry, has been beaten and left for dead as he sought to bring the Gospel to the villages of radical Hindus and Muslims. I must tell you, I am so drawn by the fire of God that I see in this man. When I look into Dr. Paul's eyes, I see Jesus.

I love this man.

I believe in this man.

I don't know anyone in the world who is more used by God today than Dr. K.A. Paul. He and Gospel to the Unreached Millions have a blueprint that can thrust out national workers from the 10-40 Window countries to these diverse nations, cultures and languages at a fraction of what it costs to send Western missionaries.

God is raising up a great ocean of willing national Christian leaders who are ready to finish the task. They need the resources and prayer of the West to enable them to go. Would you prayerfully consider joining us to finish this great task?

From His Excellency,
The Mayor of Kurnool Municipal Corporation

To Dr. K.A. Paul:

It is really gratifying that you have conducted a crusade in our city from 19th to 23rd February, 1997. This was a mammoth festival where Christians and non-Christians in millions have gathered in the widest grounds of this city.

The crusade is so great that never in the history of this city or state people have gathered in such great numbers under one banner. Words are not enough to think of and praise the mightiness that has been attempted by you and the way our city has been blessed.

It is my pleasant duty and privilege to express my heartful thanks on behalf of the citizens irrespective of religion, caste and creed. The great and whole hearted ambition of all the citizens of our city is your early return.

Souls over 800 thousand! Oh, if I could really count nearly one million have accepted Christ as their personal Savior through your message. I am one among them and I am the witness for this great harvest. Persistence and endurance are greatly essential. Kindly do the needful by raising native missionaries to reach the unreached millions.

With kind regards,
Yours Sincerely,
Bangi Ananthaiah

LEFT FOR DEAD
K.A. PAUL OF INDIA

Chapter 1--Left For Dead

Each thudding smash from a dozen angry fists, brass knuckles and wooden rods seemed to break hundreds of the slender threads knitting my spirit to my body. I fought for consciousness as hard as my assailants were trying to pound it from me.

Now they yanked at my hair. Perhaps they would pry off the top of my head, and my spirit would zoom out. I fell repeatedly, my body slippery with its own blood and the spittle of my enemies. I tried to scamper between the legs of my tormenters, but one grabbed me.

"You can't escape this time!" he yelled.

"This is your day to die!" shrieked another.

NO FAREWELLS

I would die without saying farewell to my father or mother, brother or sister. My mind fled to thoughts of them, hoping their emotional arms would be there to succor me as they had so often. My dad had only reluctantly consented for me to try to preach Jesus Christ in Orissa State of my native India. How sad he would be when they plopped my body at his doorstep in Vishakapatnam, in neighboring Andhra Pradesh State. Years earlier, he himself had been delivered from madness. How ironic that madmen would now slaughter his son.

My spirit yearned to fly to Heaven, to be with Jesus. My arms strained at their sockets as two hefty enemies of my Lord dragged me out to a ditch. A trail of blood followed, gushing from my mouth. My bones showed just under my dark skin, ridges on the barren landscape of my thin, tortured body.

Consciousness finally–mercifully–took flight. One of the men placed his rough, bloody hands around my neck and squeezed until my body went limp.

"He is dead. Leave him," he said.

And so they left me in the ditch–for dead.

Sometime earlier the fanatics had taken note of me, and this had led to the beating. I had come to the village I will call Palli, in Orissa State, to bring the people the Gospel of Jesus Christ. I had walked out of the surrounding jungle one day into this tiny hamlet with its crystal clear stream. It danced down through the hills, and the villagers had dammed up the waters, and found them to have a pleasant taste. But I wanted to bring them Water of Life to quench their inner thirst forever.

SUCCESS ATTRACTS ATTENTION

From the lush green hills, I could look down on the tile-roofed huts of Palli. They were made of unfired brick. I had preached there several times, and I knew that inside those huts were many new disciples of Jesus. We had even been able to plant a church there. Many of the people had openly followed Christ, allowing themselves to be baptized in water for all to know.

This is what had caught the attention of the fanatics. Each time they saw me in town, they would argue with me over religion and spiritual matters. The confrontations were more heated each time. The leader of the gang–whom I will call Vic– would be especially incensed. I would make my case, but he and his friends refused to listen.

But there were many others who did. My usual rounds in Palli took me to four homes for Bible study. On a particular evening, one of the houses was crowded with 30 people. I preached on one of my favorite topics, the story of Zacchaeus.

While it seemed only minutes, I had talked for three hours. Heaven had opened over that little hut, and everyone inside was being bathed in its joy and freshness. But now it was 10:30 p.m., and time to send the people home.

However, in the meantime, a crowd had gathered outside. Quiet at first, the restless people began to get unruly. Someone started a chant, and before long the whole mob had picked it up. "Come out!" they yelled. "This is your day! Come out or we will break down the door!"

POUNDING FISTS

The door throbbed with their pounding fists. To me, the bumping was a percussion summons to death. Now the angry people rattled the windows of the little house. The church members inside did not count their lives as dear to themselves, and were protecting me without regard to their personal safety. But I knew the small number inside the house would soon be overwhelmed by the mob outside. The door of the mud hut was quaking. This must have been the scene when the lust-crazed crowd at Sodom assaulted the house of Lot. This marauding army at Palli was driven, not by sexual desire, but by a lust for my blood.

If God didn't intervene soon, not only would my life be in danger, but those with me as well. I had seen God do miraculous things. For a moment, I became a "son of thunder," and considered calling down fire on my enemies.(Luke 9:54) But the Voice of the Spirit, in its quiet authority, was louder than the fearful
shriek of the sons of thunder. If I entered the coming ordeal with the willingness to forgive my opponents, God said, He would guide me through the situation.

Two church members who were among Palli's most respected men, went out to try to reason with the mob, whose leader was a man I will call Vic.

"We told him not come back!" someone yelled at the church leaders. "Why has he come again?"

Now Vic spoke. "This man is creating problems. Many of our people are following him. We have to stop this."

"Kill him!" went up the cry from members of the crowd.

The Christian leaders stared at Vic and his accomplices. "If you want to kill this young man, kill us first. Then you can kill him."

ANGELIC MINISTRY

I have no doubt these men were standing in some of the authority with which Jesus faced down an angry mob at Nazareth. (Luke 4:30) "Angel" literally means "messenger." God's angels are ministering spirits to His servants. (Hebrews 1:13-14) The words of the church leaders were as angels from God before the mob, and the mob quieted. The men came back into the house, and we prayed and cried to God until midnight. Finally, the crowd backed away.

They could not touch me until God's time.

As they backed away, someone cried, to his allies, "If this man comes here again, we will cut off one his legs, tie him to a tree, then kill him!" The rest cheered, and then scattered to their homes. But their words lingered in my soul, along with the sense of the powerful malevolence behind them.

In the house, we thanked God and waited for the last of the crowd to leave. Then the church members escorted me out of town, and I plunged into the breath-stealing darkness of the surrounding jungle. I spent the subsequent days studying again the Book of Acts, and being strengthened by remembering how God had directed the steps of the Apostles, and how the Father had protected Peter and Paul. I was comforted, because I knew He would protect me. I might suffer stripes, but I knew no one

could take my life from the world until God gave permission.
    But now, to human eyes staring down at my bleeding body in the ditch, I appeared to be lifeless.

LEFT FOR DEAD
K.A. PAUL OF INDIA

Chapter 2--Venkata Rao Becomes 'Barnabas'

Almost three decades earlier, it had been my father who was surrounded by terrifying forces that were seeking his death. My father had been encircled by the powerful demons of a religious system in which he was a leader.

Dad was not huddled in a mud hut, as I was. His torment was in his own home. Low-hanging clouds made that night in 1963 darker than usual. A storm swept in off the Bay of Bengal. Lightening and thunder exploded over the house where my father, Venkata Rao, tried to sleep. Fitfully, he would awaken, and watch the brilliant flashes through the skylight of the house.

TWIRLING STORM

Suddenly, a bolt seemed to thrust through the roof and into my father's chest. The thunder seemed to crash down on him as if it had chosen him for special torment out of all the beings on earth. Fear, anxiety, distress now became the elements of a storm blowing and tearing inside my father's heart.

Fearing he was losing control, Venkata Rao got up from the bed. He frantically walked through the house, trying to reassure himself that he had not been struck physically, that all was well. But it was not. A dread had formed in him like the remnant of a bleak, twirling storm cloud that would not fade away. The thunder and lightning stopped outside, but not in the heart of my father. He could not help himself. He wondered who would deliver him from the torment.

Venkata Rao was trained as a chemist and doctor. As quickly as possible, he downed all the medicine he could. Yet the torment of fear, dread and anxiety would not leave. He sought specialists in physiology and psychology. But no one could send the fresh breeze that would dissipate his inner torture. Finally, his condition was threatening to him and our whole family.

From a human perspective, there seemed to be little reason for my father's growing insanity. My parents were natives of Saripalli in the State of Andhra Pradesh. It is a small village cradled in the lap of tree-blanketed hills. When the monsoon comes, the dry creek bed becomes a raging river, making the hamlet almost inaccessible. But the rains nourish the rich growth of mangoes and oranges grow right in our yard.

RESPECTED 'GURU'

My parents are *Kapus*–one of the highest castes in India. I had been born that same year–September 25, 1963. By every human standard, I was birthed into a comfortable, upper middle class family in a spacious house refreshed by a continual sea-breeze.

However, my father and mother were Hindu idol worshippers, believing in some three million false gods. They could pick and choose their gods. Snakes, cows, moneys, trees, rivers, the stars, the moon, the sun, all are candidates for godhood in the Hindu system. For a Hindu like my father, almost everything he could see he could turn into a deity. Human beings were worshipped–even demons. My father was among people who offer sacrifices to whatever person, object or spirit they choose. Dad was also a respected guru in the local Hindu community, and served part time as a priest at the temple. His name–prior to his conversion to Christ–*Venkata Rao*, was that of a familiar Hindu deity.

So, to try to escape his torment, Venkata Rao went to temples and made many sacrifices and offerings. He went to be baptized in a river regarded as holy by Hindus, called *Papa Nashanam*. He took my brother, sister and me down into the waters with him. I was barely a toddler, and I am thankful dad didn't lose me in the rushing flow. Many small children has drowned in such rituals. There was nothing my dad left out from his knowledge as a Hindu, with mother was at his side.

My parents visited all the temples and shrines they could. They went to the Venkateswara temple—the one built to honor the god for whom my dad was named. There, people wait for days for just a moment's visitation from the deity. But even though dad bore the name of this god, the deity was silent. Father and mother were realizing that nothing they did meant anything. Chanting prayers was like speaking to a dead person. There was no response, though my parents cried out to their favorite gods. All temples and shrines lost meaning to my father and mother.

CONFRONTING REALITY

Though they did not know the Bible, my parents were coming face to face with the reality of Psalm 115:5-7, which says,

> They have mouths, but they cannot speak; they have eyes, but they cannot see; They have ears, but they cannot hear; they have noses, but they cannot smell; They have hands, but they cannot feel; they have feet, but they cannot walk; they cannot make a sound with their throat.

My mother's birth name was Sanyasamma, meaning, "isolated from the world." It signifies a female who does not chase material things. Very religious, my mother would fast and pray to her favorite Hindu god three times a week. She was the cherished only child of her family. Because of a birth defect, she had a twisted tongue, which caused many problems for her at school as a child. Her parents had withdrawn her from school at a young age because of the torment of the other children. But God later taught her to read without human help.

Marriages are often arranged in India, so my grandparents brought together my father and mother. Though raised in the same village, they had had no contact with one another. People in the village were worried about the match. My father was already known as a cruel, angry man, while my mother was noted for her calm, quiet naivete.

DEMONIC TORMENT

In Ephesians 4, the Spirit inspires Paul to warn people about the huge ground that can be given to demons through anger. The Apostle writes:

> Be ye angry, and sin not: let not the sun go down upon your wrath: Neither give place to the devil. (Ephesians 4:26-27, KJV)

My dad was under profound demonic torment because the enemy had found in him the ample ground of anger. What had produced it?

Father has two brothers and three sisters. All the brothers are well educated. One even has a PhD., and teaches in a senior college operated by the government. Dad also was highly trained. However, he was forced to stop his climb to the top academic level when his father died. My dad had to drop out of school, and, as the oldest son, support the family. He worked long hours from a young age to support the others. His schooling was cut off, but he enabled the others to go on, and watched them as they received high degrees and much prestige.

My dad's anger was often directed against Christians. His pharmacy practice took him to Chittivalsa, a town 20 kilometers from Saripalli. He was attached to a company called Jute Mills, where thousands are employed. The company provided a house for our family. Ironically, it was in the middle of a group of Christian homes. This is also miraculous, part of God's sovereign plan for our family, since even today in India, there is less than one evangelical Christian for every 100 people.

God, in His great sovereign act--and humor--put us in a house directly across from a mission church, sponsored by a group from London. My parents had asked the Jute Mill authorities for another house--anywhere. Their request was denied, with the Jute Mill management no doubt controlled by Higher Authority they knew nothing about.

'MOST STUPID RELIGION'

"Christianity is the most stupid religion," dad would rail. "They say only people they think are holy will go to Heaven, and all the rest will go to hell." Father would be fierce as he drove deeper, asking Christians, "How come you teach that Jesus is the only way to God where there are many gods and prophets?" Then he would preach to them: "Our Hindu religion is broad-minded. We believe in everything. All the ways and religions will lead to the same goal and Heaven. You Christians get American money and spread your religion and convert people to it!"

One of his work-mates was a pharmacist, Mr. Charles, a solid, upright follower of Jesus. Dad argued with him constantly. Sadly, some of father's points were valid. "If you say you are the only people going to Heaven, why don't you Christians have a different lifestyle? We have drinks, and Christians drink ... smoke ... gamble ... steal. The only difference I know is we Hindus worship many gods and you worship only Jesus. That is the only difference!"

Mr. Charles would always answer with soft patience. He was constantly seeking ways to show love to dad and our whole family. He prayed for us frequently. My father closed his eyes to Christians like Mr. Charles, who lived Christlike lives. Dad was so bitter, he started Hindu Sunday services. He invited friends to our house across from the church. Father would play his harmonium, and the others *sitars*, harp-like *vinas*, drums, tambourines. They would make such loud noise with the instruments that the Christians couldn't worship in peace.

DEITY 'ASLEEP'?

It has been estimated there are 330 million gods in the Hindu pantheon: gods of four-footed animals and bugs; gods of families and villages; gods of places; gods of rain and thunder. Though she had never heard of Paul's words to the Athenians in Acts 17:23, when my father became ill, my mother was so desperate she called to the "unknown God." All the good advice from doctors, medicines and temples proved a failure. Elijah taunted the priests of Baal with the suggestion their god was asleep. My parents realized the situation was worse than that: the gods they had trusted weren't even alive. My father and mother were being deprived of physical life, and now their spiritual being was crushed as well.

Dad's life became hell on earth, intolerable. One day as he sat before his favorite meal of shrimp curry and rice, the lightning and thunder returned. Shaken by panic and dismay, he stopped eating. The thunder would probe to the deep hiding places of his heart and crash in, destroying everything. Desperate, deadly fear blasted through him like lightning bolts.

One of the reasons dad had wanted wealth was to build his own movie theaters, a dream he never realized. He spent hours watching films. He especially enjoyed one in our Telugu language, called *Patala Bairavi*. Its chief character was a hellish god, and the movie entertained with Sufi dancing and Hindu music that greatly pleased father. Now, in his madness, he sought out a favorite cinema. Perhaps he could hide from the thunder in the darkness of a movie theater, his tormented mind thought. He almost moved into the cinemas. One night he was even asked to leave because the theater was closing and the building was being locked.

DESTROYING IDOLS

In our house was a "god room." Inside were numerous wooden idols, images made of silver and mud, and pictures of Hindu deities. So much incense had been offered in the room through the years, it had penetrated into the walls as a permanent scent. Venkata Rao spent hours in the room, crying to the gods for deliverance. He didn't understand he was asking relief from the very demons bringing his torment. Finally, he decided to destroy all those images his ancestors had worshipped for generations. He screamed, "If there is truly any god, why would I suffer the way I am suffering?"

As an idol-worshipping Hindu, my father dreaded death as much as life. Now, my parents came to the conclusion there were no gods in Hinduism. Dad became a theist. He had a vague belief in a Higher Power, but the Divine was unknowable, uncaring, untouchable. At last, not even theism sufficed, and dad became an atheist.

Dad decided that he feared death less than living. He explained to my mother he preferred to die. "I can take no more of this; please let me die," he pled. But what about the family. Who would care for mother, and the children? My father proposed suicide for the whole family. Sadly, my mother agreed. Dad made the necessary arrangements. He acquired poisons, and began mixing a solution we would all take and collapse simultaneously.

Family suicide may be a strange notion to Westerners. But in India, children obey parents, irrespective of age. In ancient times, we had a joint family system, in which all property was held in common by all the relatives, akin to the early church pattern. Women obey their husbands, and live amicably with in-laws. Thus, for my father to leave his family was almost unthinkable. The family would go with him--even in death.

MR. CHARLES

As my father mixed the deadly solution, my mother suddenly had a thought. Mr. Charles, my dad's work-mate, with whom he argued so often, she recalled, was a Christian who had tried to tell my parents about Christ's Way. Suddenly, somehow she knew that they must contact Mr. Charles before going any further with the suicide plan. She grabbed the vial of poison and ran to find Mr. Charles.

On hearing what was about to happen, Mr. Charles immediately sought help for my family from a pastor, whose name happened to be the same as the great reformer, Martin Luther. Instead of leading his family to suicide, my father submitted to counseling by Pastor Luther. As my dad received Pastor Luther's ministry, the evil time faded. The devil and his demons retreated from my father. God's message of hope took deep root in both my parents. They were a perfect example of the fact that when God's Word enters and is received, the opposite spirit has no place to stand in a person's life. My father and mother received the promise that Jesus Christ would bring relief. Pastor Luther told them, "Jesus Christ died for you that you need not die." For the first time, my parents found real hope.

How did my family come to God? No doubt, God's own sovereignty was at work. It pleased God to afflict my father and thus make it possible for us all to embrace Christ, in Whom we found rescue and healing. Perhaps it was also my mother's crying out to the "unknown God" that found the Heart of the God Who makes Himself known through Jesus. It was the LORD Who instructed His 70 witnesses to find the "man of peace," who would receive their message, in villages they would visit, and lodge with that person. (Luke 10:6) Through the tribulation, my father and mother had become a man and woman "of peace." My parents also illustrate the fact that when people without the Gospel yearn for God, somehow He will get them to the place of receiving the Gospel.

DUMBFOUNDED

As Pastor Luther counseled my father, dad thought of the old ways. What would this God want? As a Hindu, my father knew one had to sacrifice to the gods. "You need not give Jesus anything," Pastor Luther said. "In fact, He wants to give you something–eternal life!" My father was dumbfounded. "You have prayed to all the gods but the true and living One," said Pastor Luther. Then he invited Venkata Rao to church.

Meanwhile, father reflected on Christ. He accepted the invitation to church, and even took his music instrument to help with the songs. My dad was touched deeply in every sense. His hope soared. The church building was a small hut, and there were only four people in the congregation. The pastor was a poor man, living in poverty. Dad wondered why someone would serve under such difficult circumstances. He watched as the congregation would pray fervently on their knees. Sometimes they clapped, sometimes they lifted up their hands toward Heaven, talking to God. The people seemed to speak to Someone Who was visibly present. Dad couldn't get over it. It was genuine, real, in contrast to all the empty ritual he had known. He sense these people really did have relationship with God. They prayed in tears for my father, and his hope shot up even higher.

Dad had opportunity to think and rethink about his life and the new revelations pouring in. He had no idea a global ministry would grow out of the decisions he would make during those days. He kept attending the church, playing music. At one service, it was announced there would be fasting and prayer for three days, from 6 a.m. until midnight. During that period, the people did not sing, but they prayed and wept. On the second day, my parents lost interest in food. The main theme of the prayers was the healing of my father and blessing for our whole family.

CONVICTED

Conviction began to settle upon my father. He realized he was hot tempered and cruel. He surrendered to whims and fancies. These practices, he saw, were not compatible with his new faith in Christ. The Holy Spirit lifted the veil on my dad's soul, and he saw his sin. What he had previously considered normal and natural he now viewed as opposed to the righteousness of God. He had been so hard to live with, my mother had once wanted to jump into a well and end her life. Though at the time she was a heathen, she heard a sweet Voice saying, "One day your husband will change and your future will be peaceful and pleasant." Now the promise was being fulfilled as my dad moved in repentance.

In fact, my father experience a "movie" of his sinful life, played out on the screen of his mind. He also saw clearly that Christ had taken the penalty of that evil life on the cross. With no delay, Venkata Rao asked Jesus to be his Savior. At last he found complete relief. Peace and joy flooded through him, driving out the thunder and terrorizing storms of the psyche. He began singing, *every sin has to go, 'neath the crimson flow ...*

My father, Venkata Rao, was now a Christian. As he was returning home, just to prove to my father the awesome reality of his new life, God sent a storm. The rain fell in driving torrents. Thunder boomed around dad, and lightning flared furiously. But that meant nothing to this new man in Jesus Christ. In fact, my father was so deeply "hidden" in Christ he wasn't even aware of the weather which had previously terrorized him. He was completely delivered in spirit, soul and body.

AWESTRUCK

And so was our family. As my father was falling under conviction, so was my mother. She was absolutely certain that Jesus Christ is Lord. She began tearing off her idol-jewelry, as she "put on" the Lord Jesus Christ. Jewelry means everything to a Hindu woman, and it takes the power of Christ to cause her to throw away the trinkets and charms. The change in mother was visible to the world. She was in tune with her husband. It had been out of ignorance that they had been idol-worshippers, but now the Word of God had driven out the ignorance and brought them Light. They were awestruck at each other's conversion to Christ.

Salvation had come to our house. My parents took extreme care to raise their children in the ways of Christ. Our whole household began to serve the Lord. Nearby villages began to ring with the news of my father's conversion to Christ. Scores of little towns were hearing that Christ had come to a Hindu couple. My parents' changed lives were the best witness. The fact that Jesus saves from sin and heals the body became the main topic of conversation in many neighboring villages. Hundreds accepted Christ and began attending church. Like

Zacchaeus of old, my father began to return items he had stolen.

My dad had to change his name. As a follower of Christ, he could no longer carry the name of a Hindu idol. He was no longer Venkata Rao, but *Barnabas*. Immediately, our Hindu relatives severed relations with us. My father's brother took away family property. But my dad sang,

> *All that I want is in Jesus.*
> *He satisfies, joy He supplies.*
> *Life would be worthless without Him.*
> *All things in Jesus I find ...*

My father brought up his children to know the Lord. He taught us to live Biblical lifestyles. He taught us to put God above all else. He himself lived as an example to us, never exchanging spiritual things for the worldly. He became a godly father. My brother, David Raju, my sister, Krupa, and I were all brought up to serve Christ and His Kingdom. It is as if we came into the world with a specific Divine task and purpose. We have nothing apart from God and serving Him.

And dad himself took on the mantle of ministry after his conversion. He began to evangelize villages and pioneered a church. Many Hindus, on hearing of father's healing, went away healed themselves. Physical healing led them to spiritual healing.

Today, I honor my parents, and feel a great debt to them. Our spiritual up-bringing superseded even that of most in the Western "Christian" world. This is because my parents were sold out for Christ. There was no compromise. Their world view was determined by their heavenly focus. They believed in Christian education, and knew the balance between love and discipline. They knew their parental responsibility before God. They inspired us to serve Him.

LEFT FOR DEAD
K.A. PAUL OF INDIA

Chapter 3--A Christian Home In India

My parents took their new life with utmost seriousness. They were determined to establish a Christian home midst all the paganism of our society.

In fact, they were so concerned for their children's spiritual development that they considered sports and play as of little value. They felt such things would retard our spiritual growth.

Yet our parents weren't mean, even if their attitudes seemed legalistic. In fact, my dad's new name, "Barnabas," was most appropriate. He encouraged us constantly, and was gentle though direct in his discipline. He used neither rod nor harsh words, but always led us by his sheer example. Before my dad met Christ, he was the opposite. But the change in his personality is a powerful testimony of the ability of Christ to make a person brand new.

USE TIME WISELY

Against my parents' wishes, I plunged into school sports. I was a fast runner--a quality that would help me later in my ministry--and won prizes for racing. As I grew, I realized that play and sports are not in themselves evil. Paul the Apostle loved racing, and illustrated his teaching sometimes with examples from sports. Followers of Christ must be balanced in their priorities. Time needs to be properly proportioned. My father taught me that persons with high callings in the Kingdom especially need to be alert to the best use of time.

Samuel is an example. He had the call of God in his life

from the womb. His people were in great spiritual need, and Samuel found little time for anything but ministering to them. The same was the case of John the Baptist, who had the high ministry of preparing the way for Jesus' earthly ministry. In modern times, C.T. Studd, the great English sportsman, laid aside his fame and fortune as a champion cricket player, and used his wealth to fund his and others missionary ministries. Balance is found in looking at Jesus. He allowed nothing to interfere with ministry, even things that appeared to be urgent and good.

Balance is lost when sports and entertainment become idols. This grieves the Holy Spirit, my father taught me. He helped me see that many Christians are feasting rather than fasting, playing, but not praying, laughing instead of lamenting for souls.

UNCOMPROMISING

My father was uncompromising on spiritual issues, even when it seemed to promise loss or harm. While he was working as a pharmacist, Sunday was a holiday in India, a remnant of British rule. Later, Sunday was declared a work day. A factory might have 100 Christians among several thousand Hindu employees. Most of the Christians worked on Sunday, fearing they would be fired. But not my dad. To him, Sunday was a special day for the Lord. He was asked by officials for an explanation of his beliefs and actions. He told them Sunday was a holy day and he spent it in God's presence. God gave my father favor with those authorities, and they made Sunday an off-day for all Christians.

Dad won a great victory that day. In his stand for Christ, he reminded me of Daniel in Babylon. The prophet wouldn't bow his knee to a false god, nor would Daniel give up his special time of prayer.

One of the things that happened each Sunday was home

church. We gathered at 6 a.m., and worshipped for an hour. Then we went into the streets and market places to distribute Christian literature. Finally, we would attend a Gospel meeting until 10 p.m.

My father not only came to believe with all his heart, but live by his faith with complete abandon. He became a model churchman. I watched him practice sacrificial stewardship, giving far behind his tithe. Sometimes, he seemed to give, not just 10 percent, but double his total income. He was also an example in prayer, fasting and evangelizing.

Our close ties to the local church brought me across the path of some great men of God who imparted into my life. Pastor Martin Luther was followed by Pastor Rao, who, with my father, taught me much about prayer. God used Pastors Mathews, Kasulamma and Mohan to mold my life and fill it with the Word of God.

WATER BAPTISM

Finally, there came the wonderful day when I was baptized in water at a Christian convention at Visakhapatnam. Though decades have passed, that day is still special to me. Water baptism is a person's open separation from the world and to God. While I do not believe that baptism itself saves, I do believe it is essential if one is going to go deeper with Jesus. He commanded that we be baptized. Thus, to refuse or neglect water baptism is to disobey Jesus. To disobey Him is to place oneself in the position of missing out on some of His greatest blessings. Many people shun water baptism because they want to be "secret" Christians. Such a concept is a contradiction! In a society like India, with fervent Islam, burning Hinduism and many other religions and cults, open identification with Jesus Christ can be dangerous. But to not take the open stand is an act of rebellion and a quenching of faith.

As I grew in the Lord, listening at the feet of my pastors, following Jesus, I experienced His Voice within me. Jesus was my unseen Teacher. He always travelled with me. I felt His Presence. God met my needs as a lad. I laid hands on the sick and oppressed and asked Jesus to heal them, and He did. He was as real to me as if He were still present in His earthly Body.

Saturday was a day of preparation. We fasted and prayed every Saturday until midnight. While these activities might seem extreme to some Christians, one must remember what my father and mother were saved from. They had gone from profound darkness to dazzling Light. They wanted to spend every moment in that Light, and lead their children to do the same.

STRENGTH FOR HARDSHIP

These were also days of preparation for the ministry God to which God was calling me. The lifestyle of our family became rooted in my subconscious mind. It strengthened me for the difficult task of evangelizing among people who would want to kill me. The family lifestyle prepared me for long, hard hours, sleepless nights, wearying jetlag, and all the other challenges I would face as an evangelist to the nations.

In fact, being associated with my earthly father's business meant doing my Heavenly Father's business. The business of God's Kingdom was and is my earthly dad's enterprise. He understands well the parable statement of Jesus that His people are to "occupy" until He comes. (Luke 19:13) Literally, "to occupy" in New Testament Greek means "to do business." Jesus was telling His disciples that rather than withdrawing and waiting for His Return, they were to be doing the "business" of the Kingdom of God.

Thus, my earthly father was doing his Heavenly Father's business. I, in turn, gave myself over to my earthly father's business, which meant that at the same time I was doing my

Heavenly Father's business! This is an awesome model of fatherhood. It is exactly what Jesus did. "I only do what I see My Father doing," He said. (John 5:19) The finest godly human dad is one his child can imitate, and in doing so, the child does the will of the Heavenly, Eternal Father.

All three of my father's children are on "daddy's business." We serve in Gospel to the Unreached Millions ministry. I became a Christian when I was a six-year old lad. From that time on, I was introduced to and trained in father's business, learning to do *the* Father's Business.

Father preached and I sang. I also preached, sometimes quoting verses from the Hindu scriptures--the *Vedas*--which asserted that blood had to shed for remission of sin, and that God has to come down from above. This, of course, coincides with the Bible, and opened the door for witness to Hindus. I then told the audience that all this was fulfilled in the Blood of Christ.

DRUNKARDS AND ATHEISTS

As a "boy preacher" I spoke in many open air meetings. Often, my father and I had to outrun drunkards and atheists who chased us. Once, dashing away from maddened people, we almost fell into a well whose entrance was grown over and not visible. Another time, we almost ran face to fang with a writhing cobra snake. In some villages, in addition to the drunkards and atheists, we had to deal with antagonistic Hindus and Muslims. But always, there were those who gave their lives to Christ, and that made our afflictions worth it all.

We preached a positive message. Rather than criticizing the false gods the people worshipped, we made great effort to address the spiritual needs of the people. A personal concern for the spiritual welfare of people creates successful, effective communication of the Gospel. So, instead of saying negative things about their false gods, we carefully explained the Good News of Jesus, and shared what He had done for us. Then the audiences began to see the clear distinctives between Jesus and their idols. In that brilliant contrast, their hearts became open to the Gospel.

Love was always the atmosphere in which my father taught me to minister. He taught me how Christ loves the people. Rather than attacking the religious beliefs of people, we preferred to share His love, forgiveness, healing power, deliverance. Many times, we saw proof of the fact that if we lift up Christ, "He will draw all men unto Himself." (John 12:32)

CHRIST'S UNIQUE WAY

All the world's religions deal with how people can placate God and get on His "good side" so they won't experience wrath. Millions of people are bound up in these religious systems, feverishly trying to atone for their own sins, and do enough good deeds to save themselves. Only in Christ does God do it all for us. This means all religions are law-based; but Christ's way is based on grace. God says, "you must be holy as I am holy." That's all religion hears, and adherents try to make themselves as holy as God. But in Christ, God *gives* us His holiness, if we will receive it. When people buried under crushing religious loads hear this, it is glorious "good news" to them. This is why it is called "Gospel."

The world's religions also start with man, rather than with God. That is, a person follows a certain religion because he thinks it will bring him good luck, wealth and health. Such a person doesn't follow God because God is holy and deserves man's complete adoration, but only for what he perceives God might do for him. Only in Christ do we see the way that begins with God, His holiness and His love. This causes a person to focus away from himself or herself, to fix the gaze on God as the priority. The secondary result is that such a person gets focused on the needs of other people in greater way than his own needs.

Because I was a "boy preacher" many people took interest. Once, a mob of 300 faced me and began to fire questions at me, a mere lad. Jesus had told His disciples that

> "when they arrest you and deliver you up, do not be anxious beforehand about what you are to say, but say whatever is given you in that hour; for it is not you who speak, but it is the Holy Spirit." (Mark 13:11)

God fulfilled that promise that day. I was no theologian nor religious expert. Yet by God's grace I answered all their queries. The mob dispersed, satisfied.

'ASSIMILATING' JESUS

Through experiences like this I learned that people really do not hate Jesus. In fact, in India they sometime honor Him as another of their gods. While we do not want them to hate Him, we certainly don't want to encourage them to see Jesus simply as an "add on" to their list of idols. So we preach that He is the *only* way of salvation. It is probably also true in the West that often people are not rejecting Jesus, but our representations of Him. Or, they attempt to conform Him to their lifestyle, instead of repenting and truly following Him. This is why it is important to preach the grace of Jesus, but also the clear claim that He is the only Savior, and the definite demand that we are to follow Him rather than trying to make Him follow us.

My father and I would see missionaries and evangelists come to India from the outside. They would conduct big crusades with much fanfare, and report to their supporters back home that hundreds–sometimes thousands–had accepted Christ.

But we knew that usually the large crowds that responded were already Christians. When non-Christians responded, it would be in response to calls for healing.

So, when an Indian national preaches, he will not simply quote Scriptures and use Biblical language the Indian crowds do not understand. We Indian evangelists know we must make clear that Jesus is the only way to the Father, otherwise the people will simply incorporate Him into their catalogue of false gods. In fact, we have to get specific, addressing the issue of having multiple gods, and the practice of idolatry. Yet, as I noted above, we must do this in a non-critical, loving manner.

A SAVIOR NEEDED

No Hindu understands that he is a sinner. He recognizes his life is under continual assault, but he believes this is because of evil spirits. He doesn't understand that his own sin gives ground for the operation of powers of darkness, nor that it cuts him off from his loving Heavenly Father. So we have to convince them of sin and the need for a Savior. Gently, lovingly, breaking down the Hindu world view and presenting the Bible's perspective is vital. So we demonstrate the need, show that man is helpless to meet it, and then flood that gap of need with the truth of the Gospel.

The Word of God is a living power. When it is presented under the anointing of the Holy Spirit, it goes into the heart of a person and does the work of convicting and inviting to Christ. Yet this is why a native Indian can be more effective than a well-meaning foreigner who gives words to which the Indian cannot relate. The Indian evangelist understands the world view that must be addressed,a nd that must be shown to be inadequate. Also, when the Indian evangelist preaches to the lost, the people do not connect the message with materialistic issues. Rather, they focus on the spiritual. When Jesus is preached through an

Indian heart to an Indian heart, He is not perceived as a foreign God.

This is not to say that non-Indians are not needed in India. In fact, the opposite is true. We need much help in training pastors and leaders for the planting of churches. In fact, we in India realize we cannot do this without help. The best use of the ministry gifts of non-Indians is in conducting leadership seminars, assisting financially with establishment and support of churches to care for the great harvest, and intercession.

We urgently need the help of Christians from throughout the world who are experienced in church leadership. After crusades, my father taught me to do follow-up. Local churches are flooded with new people. While the native evangelist and missionary can be more effective in evangelism than the non-Indian, it takes that person from outside to help us establish the churches that can handle the harvest. I always take non-Indian pastors and other leaders with me on crusades to help train our leaders. The task of establishing local churches is urgent. Such churches are like silos, ready to receive the grain. If the silo is not built, the grain spoils. Without strong local churches, tender young believers are easy prey for the spoiling work of the evil one.

APPRECIATION FOR MISSIONARIES

It is also important for we non-Westerners to give God thanks for the missionaries and evangelists who came to us with the Gospel. Many gave the ultimate sacrifice, dying to get the Gospel to India. All made the sacrifice of family, home and friends to come and live among us. Foreign missionaries perform a catalytic work. They seed the Gospel in a place. Then it becomes the responsibility of we who live in the nations to cultivate that seed, and plant it throughout our homelands.

I received much blessing and guidance from outside

preachers and missionaries. When I was nine, an American pastor prophesied that I was called to the unreached peoples of the world, while another declared that God was preparing me for a great purpose and harvest. Yet another made it even more specific, saying that I was called especially to take the Gospel to the masses of unreached. One day while an American pastor was preaching, he paused suddenly, looked at me, and said, "you will be going to America." While I was too young to understand these words then, they have all become true.

I would have missed the destiny the messages declared had it not been for the Christian home in which I grew up. My mother was as vital to the spiritual growth of our family as my father. For two decades, she saw her primary ministry as that of a prayer warrior. She prayed and wept hours on end for lost people in communist countries as well as India. She imparted that praying spirit to me. I weep for millions passing into eternity lost, without Christ, daily.

PRAYING MOTHER

My mother prayed ardently that all three of her children would serve God. God answers prayer, but within His own time. Delays are not denials from God. Sometimes, He answers at the strike of the clock, sometimes the moment the prayer is uttered. In the Bible, Hannah asked for a child. But initially, her motives were selfish, and there was delay. In the meantime, God purified her heart. Then she made the same request out of that purity. "I will lend the child to the Lord all the days of his life," she promised. The answer came faster than e-mail.

So there were delays to my mother's petitions that all her children would be servants of the Lord, but ultimately God gave her the desire of her heart. My brother David and his wife Esther are both tireless laborers in the Kingdom of God. David, a physician, left his medical practice to work full time in ministry. My sister's husband, Yesu Padam, was a fanatic Hindu and virulently anti-Christian. He studied the Bible to find faults. Instead, the Word of God showed him he was a sinful man. He gave his life to Christ, and today writes Christian literature and serves in crusade ministry, with my sister at his side. Interestingly, his name, Yesu, is the same as "Jesus" in our language. It brings me great joy to realize that "Yesu" met the real Christ!

URGENCY FOR EVANGELISM

And for me, the combination of my father's example and my mother's intercession drilled the urgency of evangelizing into the warp and woof of my being. My heart is to reach the unreached millions. That's why we call our ministry, Gospel to the Unreached Millions. But my part of the work of GUM is just a facet of the whole. It is the vision of our whole family, and many others. Without the influence of a Christian home in India, I would not have understood the imperative urgency of Christ's call. It was He Who said, "I must work the works of Him who sent Me while it is day; the night is coming when no one can work." (John 9:4) The "day" is that period when the doors are still open to the Gospel. We must "redeem" the time, the moment of opportunity. (Ephesians 5:16) In fact, the passion of my father and mother ingrained in me the fact that all believers have an important role to play in ushering in Christ's Coming. He said, in Matthew 24:14, that the Gospel of the Kingdom will be preached in the whole world, everywhere people live, to all the nations, then the end will come.

This means all the villages of even the most remote part of my homeland will hear the Gospel of Jesus and His Kingdom. A Christian home in India is a planting, a seedling, that grows up and produces more seed. Had it not been for our neighbor, Mr. Charles, a follower of Jesus, my father would have committed suicide and taken us all with him. But in our area there was a Christian home, a planting of Jesus. Not all nations are comprised of villages. In America, there are sprawling subdivisions. In Europe, large blocks of flats. In Africa, there are huts. In Latin America, many people live in shanties. But every Christian family needs to have the vision of their home being a planting of ministry in the midst of their neighbors. My father believed the words of Joshua, when he said, "As for me and my house, we will serve the Lord." It has been true for my father's house in India, and because of it, unreached millions will hear the Good News of Jesus.

LEFT FOR DEAD
K.A. PAUL OF INDIA

Chapter 4--Journey To Hell

As I moved into my high school and college years, I almost followed an "angel of light" down the wrong road.

In 2 Corinthians 11:14, Paul writes that the devil is able to disguise himself as an "angel of light." The deceiver takes what is good, distorts it, and uses it to mislead us into his paths.

Implicit in our family's burden for the unreached millions is compassion. We feel the lostness, the pain, the confusion of our people. Jesus, our High Priest, not only knows our pains, but feels them. So, in Christ, we often experience the suffering of others around us. The devil took this impulse in me and twisted it. In high school, I became interested in politics and law. In those arenas, I thought, I could do something about the hardship of my people.

RECOGNIZED AS DISCIPLE

The school recognized me as a staunch follower of Jesus. The non-Christian teachers did not like this. But because I was born into a high caste home, they treated me respectfully. My two best friends were Brahmans. This is the highest group in India, the caste from which top leaders come. My friends believed that if they could subdue passions on this earth, and suffer for their sins in the here and now, they would attain eternal bliss. They believed they could atone for their own iniquity. They followed a religious system that knew nothing of a personal God; yet they were more sincere and devoted to their system than many who tag themselves "Christian." My friends taught me that too many of us toy with God. Perhaps this is why He does not trust us more with the great treasures of His Kingdom–like mighty works of power and miracle.

Yet I too was tempted to stray by the "angel of light." I had not learned of the illusion of political power. In my youthful idealism, I thought human institutions could solve the horrific poverty and conflict which are part of all societies. It was good to be a preacher, I knew. But it would enhance my understanding, credibility and ability to help if I were a lawyer and politician, I decided.

To pay my college bills and help support my family and father's church, I went into furniture manufacturing. As a supplier of fine woods, like teak, I prospered. We produced sofas, dining sets, beds, dressing tables. With the new prosperity, I started supporting native pastors and missionaries. My love for these special servants of God and their families grew. Later, when God called me to leave the business, it was hard because I made in three hours more money than many people made in one year in our country. Only a mighty vision could have pulled me away from my furniture business.

FORAGING IN GARBAGE CANS

One day, I visited the city of Vizayanagaram, in my home state, Andhra Pradesh. There was a huge wedding for a member of a wealthy family. It's common in India for rich people to spend much money on weddings and invite literally thousands of people. Outside the wedding house, several widows and orphans were foraging through garbage cans for the refuse left by the wedding guests. Some of the hungry children had extended bellys. In others, the ribs were visible under thin layers of skin. At the wedding feast, the food had been served on big green leaves. As the servants cleaned the tables and picked up the leaves, they would carry them to these large garbage barrels. As soon as the leaves were cast in, five or six skinny-boned children would rush over and skirmish for the leaves, which bore the scraps of leftover food. Each child had to get as many as 100 leaves to get enough remains of rice and curry to make a meager meal.

India is noted for its starving street people. But many other nations share this infamy, including America, where there are many homeless. We may wonder: Why would God allow this? In India, and throughout the world, God has created the planet with more than enough food and vegetables. The problem is in the human heart. We are to share God's blessings with one another. The beautiful order of the Kingdom of God manifested in the human heart by the Holy Spirit through the salvation won by the Son, could change the world's poverty problem in a mere moment.

MORE THAN RICE

So, when I saw the children—most of whom did not know who their parents were, but had been born and raised on the streets—I was moved to share God's love. So I took a number of them to a nice restaurant and fed them. Then I felt the need to teach them the ways of the Lord. I wanted to give them a bowl of rice that would take care of their immediate hunger. But I didn't want to give them physical food on their journey to hell, but the Gospel of salvation that lasts forever. That is why today we have ministries that care for orphans and widows as part of Gospel to the Unreached Millions—our ministry organization. Now, many of these God called us to bring in from the streets, are followers of Jesus, and spend hours in the special work of intercession, weeping and praying for the lost world. In our ministry homes, we give them bowls of rice and curry, but much more importantly, we feed them on the Bread of Life.

Though I had inklings of ministry during the time I was a prosperous businessman, I kept focused on my ultimate goal:

only as a lawyer and politician could I stop the injustice and evil I saw all around me. I did not realize that an empty-hearted politician without Jesus has nothing of eternal value to give his society. I believed that a politician with knowledge of the law could solve all the problems. I have since had the privilege of sharing the Gospel with many political leaders and officials.

My first political foray was to run for vice chairman of an important committee at our college. My friends worked hard for me, and spent much money. I gave passionate speeches on social justice. My two opponents were wealthy. I won 95 percent of the vote, making them so furious they left the college, threatening me as they went. I had been hugely successful, yet I was not in God's will. Later I would learn that success in the world doesn't always denote God's favor.

VICTORY CELEBRATION

But I didn't see such truth then, and so we threw a great victory celebration. Garlands were falling off my neck as I rose to speak again and again to the applause and cheers of my allies. In fact, they were so happy, they danced in the streets. I felt so proud and important. I was too blind to understand that whatever talents I had, God had given me for preaching the Gospel. Now I was attempting to use those gifts and abilities by own design, for my own agendas.

While I couldn't see what I was doing, my father could. A church member heard of my victory and the noisy celebrations, and told my father. I left the heady parties and went home giddy with my excitement, only to find my dad waiting for me with discipline in his eyes. Father wanted me to quit the college. In fact, he instructed the principal to terminate me as a student. I rebelled. "Whether I quit or not is my business," I told the principal. "You have no business to give heed to my father!"

For the first time, there was serious tension in our home. A spiritual struggle blazed between dad and me. He was standing for Christian principles and the calling of Christ, while I was dwindling down to lesser things. Through my self-efforts I wanted to bring justice back to the people of India. My father stood on the fact that bringing the people to Christ would solve the problems rather than mere politics. I didn't realize that the justice I was dreaming of was temporary, while my father saw the eternal Kingdom.

The only saving factor was that I continued to accompany my dad as he preached. I continued my business and college career. But being with dad as he proclaimed Christ in the streets kept me from going over totally to the world's values and methods. But one day, some of my supporters at college put it to me: "Should our great leader of the college preach in the streets?" I saw the matter from their perspective. I told my dad that I could no longer go with him into the streets because I needed the time for my studies and business. For the first time in many years, I was not at his side as he continued faithfully to preach Christ to whomever would listen.

GAINING POPULARITY

Gradually, I was gaining popularity among the 100,000 people in our town. High government officials took notice, and began attending my political meetings. Increasingly, I spoke their language. My new friends enticed me into activities which I had been taught were a waste of time--and worse. I couldn't participate and maintain active church participation, because the conflict was too great. So, I disconnected from church and the disciplines of spiritual life.

But now I faced another problem. Emptiness hollowed out my life. All the years of following Christ, finding in Him my life's meaning, and seeking to minister to the unreached, was now set aside. The new pursuits weren't big enough to fill the place once occupied by Christ. I can say now that I can't think of a worse situation than departing from Christ and His ministry. After my tryst with the world I can honestly say that it would be better not to be born than to realize the horror of emptiness without God. Many who are without God have never "tasted" His glory, and don't know the horror. Ephesians 2:12 says that to be without Christ is to be an alien from God's family, a stranger to God's promises, having no hope, and without God in the world. Lost people who've never known the Lord may not feel the depths of such lostness. But I knew. There was no place I could find shelter, no substitute I could find for the living and true God.

THE LORD INTERVENES

The Lord intervenes in a life once dedicated to Him. I began losing interest in college politics. After all, I had been exposed to the "politics"--the affairs--of the Kingdom of Heaven. Yet, as Paul wrote in Galatians, there was a struggle in me between spirit and flesh. The Kingdom of Heaven had a call on my life, yet earth had hooks in my flesh, and pulled me continually in its direction.

If college politics was too small an endeavor for me, I would launch out into the affairs of the city itself. I would be a fierce tiger of reform. I organized watchdog groups, militantly invading medical shops to ferret out their misdeeds--like selling medications after the expiration dates. Though it placed me in danger, I battled on. Once, I even took the police to a medical shop to arrest the owners, who I was certain were abusing their patients.

It used to be common in India for pharmacy shops to sell expired drugs. The uneducated villagers couldn't read, and didn't know they were consuming medications that could harm them.

It was rare for pharmacy merchants to get caught. Also, they sometimes hired the cheapest labor possible, people not qualified to work with medicines. In 1980, I moved to Narcipatnam, where my father planted a church. My brother, a physician, practiced medicine nearby. One morning, I gathered several friends from my junior college, and told them I wanted to stop the practice of selling expired medications. Some warned me not to get involved, that it could be dangerous. In fact, one of my friends knew the owner of a drug store selling the out of date medicines. He was known for his cruelty as a gang leader.

Yet, my heart was that of a young tiger, driving me to stop the injustice. So, one day, I went to the pharmacy and asked the sales person for a certain medicine. As the clerk handed me the medication, I could see it was expired. But just then he realized who I was and jerked the medicine back. Now I knew for sure this store was selling the potentially harmful medications.

THE PLAN

So, I met later with a police official and laid out a plan. On the set day, we were all ready. We sent an elderly woman to the drug store for a certain medication. As soon as the clerk sold her the medicine, some of the students and the police officer rushed in and caught the pharmacy owner, who was taken to the police station. After he was released, I lived in great danger from him, and only the grace of God delivered me from his threats.

Prostitutes feared me and my gang of moral police. Government officials were practicing bribery. We targeted one such official, and I organized rallies and demonstrations until he was removed from office. My heart burned against injustice. In my mind, I was the savior of our city. I took responsibility for stopping crime, drugs, the flow of alcohol, bribery, prostitution and anything else that smacked of wrongdoing. My heart also ached for the poor. I sought to support the native missionaries who helped people. Feeding hungry people became a passion. Despite all I did, little changed. Crime abounded, people were still hungry, injustice raged on. I was a failure.

Then God intervened. When we are set apart for the destiny He has for us, the Father will eventually cause our lives to move into situations that jar us back to His will. My dad had set me apart, and I had agreed earlier in my life. Thus, the Hand of my Heavenly Father would bring me back to the destiny spoken over me by my earthly father, with my assent.

I was troubled with the sense of failure. I could still hear a faint voice telling my that law and politics was not the answer, that only Jesus could change society by changing people, that our only hope was from above. But I resisted the voice. I didn't realize I was struggling against the Holy Spirit and His convicting power.

ON TO SENIOR COLLEGE

I finished junior college and had to move to a school where I could finish my bachelor of arts degree. At the senior college, I pursued a major in political science. My aim was to be a lawyer. One night, I attended a Gospel meeting. It disturbed my peace. I was confronted stronger than ever with the realization I could not keep running from my call to be an evangelist to the unreached millions. I tried reason: I would take the three years necessary to finish my degree, then I would return to my calling. But this line of thought was meaningless. It gave me no peace.

At 5 a.m., I was in my room, tormented. The Holy Spirit showed me that I had hacked out a path for my life that was not God's way. I begged God to leave me alone. I was deeply convicted of my backslidden condition, and my pride was wounded. I had been proud of my ability to take over my destiny. Foolishly, I thought I could improve on God's plan!

As I prayed, I began traveling in the spirit. It was in the form of a vision, yet what was happening to me felt like a literal journey. I arrived at a place where I was alone, surrounded by darkness. "God, where are you?" I screamed with bitterness. Suddenly, the darkness was overwhelmed by fiery light. I could see a vast burning lake, full of tortured people. Their cry blended into a chorale of anguish as their shrill, pain-laden voices screamed, "save me ... save me ... save me!" The cries of each individual linked with that of all the others in a maddening cacophony.

I looked around for help, and realized there was no possibility of rescue. It was like running to house aflame, knowing that it's too late to rescue the inhabitants inside. I wanted so desperately to help those flame-pierced people, but I could not. I was acutely aware that a major reason I couldn't help was because I had given up serving God.

STROLLING HEEDLESSLY TO HELL

I turned away, no longer able to look at the suffering multitudes. In the other direction, I saw another scene: People were casually going about their way, then tumbling down a deep precipice into this hell. The masses of people were strolling along heedlessly, not realizing that the very next step would be a plunge into the lake of fire. When they splashed into the flaming waves, they would realize where they were, and scream with agony, "I am in hell!"

I dashed forward trying to warn the casual wanderers. "This far and nor farther," I screamed. "Your next step is Hell. Stop! Stop! Stop! This is a dangerous place!" I tried to grab hold of people and halt them, but still many fell over the precipice into the horrible lake I had seen.

Suddenly I knew I had to find God. Only He could save

them. Again I cried, "O God, where are You?" I screamed into the darkness, "Why are these people falling?" But I couldn't find God. But I did hear a voice. "These multitudes are heading toward a lost eternity because there was no one to warn them," the voice revealed.

My vision-journey to hell went on six hours. Yet I did not feel the passage of time. All I could focus on was the reason these people were all going to hell. They must know about Jesus ... someone must tell them, I thought. At 11 a.m., my sister called me to a meal. I awoke, still trembling with fear and dread at what I had seen. I was a different man. I was abnormal. The haughty person who with the stroke of his political genius would save society was a quivering mass of tears. I wept and prayed. I couldn't eat nor sleep. I was haunted by the reality of Hell. I knew now that Hell was not a fantasy, but an awful reality.

CHANGED TOTALLY

It was some time before I could share the vision with my parents. The vision of Hell had changed me totally. I knew there was no other destiny for my life but to preach the Gospel to the unreached millions. I told my parents that I had to change. I had to deny myself, forsake my human desires, throw away my elaborate plans, give up my education, quit my business and lay down all my earthly ambitions.

I began non-stop evangelizing, irrespective of rain, heat, distance, rest, food, persecutions, exertions, or lack of transportation. I read the Book of Acts and Paul's Epistles with intensity. I could see that the Word of God had not changed; but I had. The tears kept pouring, day and night. All my future plans were shattered. Social reform, fighting corruption, all the issues that had first place in my life were pushed aside by the vision of people dropping into hell. My supreme concern was the unreached millions who did not know that perilous path they were on. I lived only to warn them. I had no time to prepare messages. I just had to spell out the danger and show the masses the answer in Jesus. When I saw the moving population on their line after line of bicycles, I could not stop preaching to them.

I came to a certain village where the people, as the Athenians in Paul's day, were worshipping an "unknown god." The people were making loud noises, thrashing about, beating themselves. Yet they found no peace, no response from their false deities. Seeing this made my heart heavy. I climbed a tree to get a broader look. Soon, the Holy Spirit released courage in me, and I scampered down the tree.

I began shouting louder, even, than the people. This got their attention. Then I began to preach the Good News. I spoke of the One God, condemned their idolatry, and told them the truth about Jesus Christ, the Son of God. Instead of receiving the message, the villagers beat me, and drove me out of their village. I returned home, weeping for them, realizing more than ever that so many people, like them, were worshipping non-living things rather than the true Savior, Who had died for them.

BEACON PASSAGE

The Word of God in Romans 15:20 became the beacon passage for my life: And so I have made it my aim to preach the gospel, not where Christ was named, lest I should build on another man's foundation ... Telling the untold, touching the untouched became the theme for the ministry to which God called me.

At last I came to terms with the fact that from childhood, God had been preparing me for the special ministry of reaching the unreached. Dad had led his children to read up to 20 chapters per day in the Bible. While Western child-rearing specialists might frown on it, father even used the Bible to discipline us. Rather than yelling at us, he would require us to read more chapters. He kept us on God's Word.

Now I understood why the Word of God was so important. As I accepted the call to the unreached millions, I discovered that often the way would be confusing and frightening, and that the only way I would know how to keep walking and what to say would be through God's Word.

LEFT FOR DEAD
K.A. PAUL OF INDIA

Chapter 5--Call To Orissa

The vision of hell changed me from being a boy preacher tagging along with his daddy into a man with an uncompromising vision. In the one night of that stark visit to the pit, I grew up.

For the first time in my life, I understood the seriousness of humanity's plight without Christ. I could no longer toy with God's calling, nor make it secondary to secular pursuits. I could not hover any longer in that gray zone between my human ambitions and the call of God. All I that I could think of was that hell is a horrible reality and only Jesus Christ can prevent human beings from going there. The ministry was not a play thing one could toss around and put down like a ball. It became for me a passionately serious matter.

THE NEXT VISION

That new understanding prepared me for the next vision God would put before me. It came at a conference of Christians I was attending in South India. One of the speakers was from Orissa State, a vast area to the north of my native Andhra Pradesh. The man spoke of the multitude of villages and deep jungle areas where the Name of Jesus had never been heard. He told the danger in Orissa. Often, missionaries and evangelists who attempted to preach there had been beaten, tortured, and, in at least one case, beheaded.

Yet, said the leader, there are 50,000 villages in Orissa State, with more than 40 million people, most were without a single church or witness. I can still hear his pleading voice as the man from Orissa quoted Hebrews 3:15: "Today if you hear His voice, do not harden your hearts ..."

In my spirit, I was hearing God's Voice. There was an intensity as I realized that Orissa would be my field of service for that period. There were many preachers in my home state. God stirred me with the sense that I was needed more in Orissa than at home. Yet I knew I had to get clarity. I began fasting and praying for further direction and guidance. I knew I had to wait on the Lord for such a strategic decision to be carried out.

Yet waiting does not mean idleness. My friend Kim and I preached and witnessed in at least 200 villages, covering many miles. My own father had ministered in some of those places. We had great joy to see the fruit of dad's previous missions. God also anointed us with deliverance ministry in those villages.

A DRUNKARD SCREAMED

In one village, a drunkard screamed at us. "Stop preaching about this Jesus," the man slurred. "You can talk about anything else you want to, but if you keep talking about Jesus we will kill you!"

We kept preaching anyway. The drunk man decided to tie us to a tree and kill us there. Yet I sensed in my spirit something great was going to happen. As the drunk went into his house to get a rope, we were surrounded by a mob. We couldn't get away if we wanted to. Kim and I began worshipping, singing loudly.

Suddenly, we heard a loud crash, but saw nothing. People in the crowd, startled by the noise, jumped--but not as high as Kim and I. The mob fell silent, as if in the presence of some awesome reality no one could see with physical eyes. The only sound was that of the drunkard, still in his house, weeping.

In a few minutes, he came out, holding a knife. Despite the ugly weapon, we felt no fear. In fact, he seemed not even to be conscious of the knife. He came straight to me, fell at my feet, and began crying out, *"Jesus Christ is the true God ... He is the truth!"*

Everyone was amazed at the change in the man. He turned to the shocked crowd. "Let these men sit down in peace," he said, motioning toward us. He brought out a coconut, hacked it open and offered us a drink from the sweet fruit. He thanked us for the message we had brought about Jesus. "Thank you for making the way of truth clear," he said. The man accepted Christ.

I couldn't help but laugh at how the devil's plot had been turned upside down by the Lord. The man who was going to tie us to the coconut tree instead gave us the rich milk of the coconut. Instead of using the knife on us, he used it on the coconut!

'I AM SOBER'

The man spoke again to the mob. "You all know me as the town drunkard," he said. "For the first time I am sober. I was bringing the rope. I was at the peak of my anger. Then suddenly, I was struck by a brilliant light. I saw the cross ...!

While the people knew almost nothing of Jesus and His way, they knew the cross was the symbol for Christ. As the man spoke, the villagers were dumbfounded. As I looked at their faces, I reflected on the fact that what had happened to Kim and me and to that formerly drunk man was for the benefit of the whole village. Now there was someone in that little town who could be responsible for ministering the Gospel of Jesus Christ-- the man who was the village drunk!

I sensed our mission there was over. Jesus once said He

had to go to the "next village." (Mark 1:38) I knew that was true for us as well. Despite the great things we experienced—like our deliverance from the drunkard—and victories in other villages, my heart still lacked the totality of peace. The call to Orissa still throbbed within me. All I could think about was the unreached of Orissa State.

Back home, I told my parents of my burden for Orissa. "Son, there is so much work to do here, and all our branch churches need your attention," said my father. So, I obeyed him, concentrating on our Telugu-speaking churches. Yet the people of Orissa were still on my mind. In fact, I couldn't help weeping for the huge tribal areas and vast jungles of the state. I was heavy laden for the unreached of Orissa.

MORE BATTLES

I now went on a special fast to pray for Orissa State. God made it clear this was my immediate field of ministry. The Holy Spirit inspired me to leave home for Orissa. Yet there were still battles in my heart. I knew no one in Orissa, and I did not speak the language. I did not have an invitation—from a human being there, at least. The Lord kept me reminding me of Abraham, who neither questioned nor doubted, but went forward out of obedience. The battle was strong.

I went back again to my parents. Feeling I had the authority of God's will, I spoke to them strongly, "I must leave for Orissa State!"

"You are in for persecution there," replied my father. "It is a dangerous place, and not many Hindus will yield to the Gospel."

"But it's impossible for me to continue here," I answered. "My heart is breaking!"

"That will pass off," dad replied.

There were a few moments of silence, my father and I

looking at each other. Then I spoke, "*I have no choice!*"

It was a terrible thing to be caught between the will of my Heavenly Father and the desire of my earthly father, whom I admired and respected as a man of God. Dad continued to state reasons why I shouldn't go to Orissa: very few churches, little support, mighty struggles. "Please don't venture into Orissa," my father pled.

"Dad, I am determined to go, because it is God's way for me," I said. I looked deeply into his eyes. "Please, let me go with your blessing," I beseeched. I turned and left, confused, full of anxiety.

I consulted Pastor Rao, my father's friend. "This is not the time to leave your father," he said. "He needs you to work with him here."

My confusion mounted. Deep inside, I knew I had to go to Orissa. Finally, miraculously, my father began to see it too. "I wanted you to be certain that it is God's will for you to go to Orissa," he told me. "If God wants you to leave for Orissa State in order to reach the unreached, who am I to hinder your progress?"

TWO CONDITIONS

Still, my dad wanted to make sure I was following God. "There are two conditions that must be met, if you desire my blessing," he said. The first was that his mother, a staunch Hindu, would accept Christ through my witness. "The second condition," he explained, "is that within a month of your arrival in Orissa, you will bring at least soul to Christ. If these conditions are met, I will be more than convinced, and you will have my blessing on the Orissa ministry."

There is an important relationship between authority, ministry anointing and submission. God will only trust His authority to those who are under authority. One day, a Roman soldier asked Jesus to heal his servant. (See Matthew 8) The warrior told Jesus that he was a man under authority, and recognized that Jesus was also under authority. Because the Roman was under the authority of Rome, he could command the resources of Rome. The soldier knew that if Jesus was under the authority of Heaven, Jesus could command Heaven's vast resources. Jesus blessed the man, because of the linkage between authority and submission.

My conflict was in the fact that my earthly dad is a godly man, who hears the Lord. Yet I knew I had a specific command from the Heavenly Father to go to Orissa. But had I defied my earthly father, who walks under the Lordship of Christ, my authority and anointing in Orissa would have been limited. Had my earthly dad been a pagan, I would have still respected him as my biological father, yet I believe I would have been free to go into Orissa despite his objection. But God has ordered the world so that those who serve Him must be submitted to other godly people, who help them hear God's Voice. Dad's blessing would be the "testimony" of another follower of Christ that I really had heard God. This would free me to go into a dangerous, needy place, with full assurance of my authority and anointing from the Holy Spirit.

WITNESS TO GRANDMA

So I sought to win grandma to Christ. First, I organized a fasting and prayer meeting at our local church. She had rejected the Gospel for 17 years. Many Hindus in Orissa would be as resistant as she. Through the years, she seemed to become more stubborn in her opposition to the Gospel. There was a sliver of hope in the fact she had not disowned us.

We invited grandma to our house. She was sitting outside our house while prayer was going on inside the church, which was nearby. I walked over to her, fell to her feet, and began weeping bitterly. "What's the matter?" she asked. "Can I help you?"

"Grandma," I said, "if you die right now, you will be going straight to hell, where there is fire and brimstone. It is a godless place. But God has not destined you for hell. Jesus Christ died to forgive you, save you and avert the bad destiny of hell. All you need to do is to receive Jesus into your heart and plead forgiveness of sins from Him. Then hell will be averted and Heaven will be your eternal future and destiny. Believe on the Lord Jesus Christ and receive your salvation!"

As I spoke, I could see grandma's resistance melting. She became convicted of her sinful condition. She went with me to the church, without delay. In front of the church members, she confessed her sins and received the Lord Jesus Christ. Even though she had seen the dramatic change in her son—my father—17 years before, she had never yielded to the Lord, until now. Our family celebrated the fact grandma was in the Kingdom with us.

"Please, baptize her immediately," I told my father. He did so, with a mixture of emotions. He was overjoyed that his mother had received the Lord, but sad because he now had to release his son to go to Orissa. So, on August 9, 1983, grandma was baptized in water, and I made arrangements to go to Orissa State.

LEFT FOR DEAD
KA PAUL OF INDIA

Chapter 6--The First of the 'Unreached Millions'

A monsoon of thoughts raged through my brain as I left home to board the train the next day for the 12-hour ride into Orissa. Torture, hardship--these were possibilities I faced. There were the biting pains of separation from my loved ones.

Yet, in the midst of it all, like the quiet eye of a hurricane, was the peace of knowing I was doing God's will, and the assurance that the life of God's obedient one is in His Hands, and not a single hair would fall from my head that He didn't permit.

I also kept wondering about the second condition for dad's blessing on my Orissa mission. Within a month, I had to win an Oriya-speaking person to Christ, though I couldn't speak the language. I knew of missionaries who had spent years learning Orissa's language and culture without winning one person.

TO ORISSA BY FAITH

On August 10, 1983--the day after my grandmother's baptism--I got on the train. I had 75-rupees--about two American dollars--a small bag of clothes, some personal items and a bicycle. There would be no one on the other end to meet me, no one to support me, no home nor church to provide me an address and roof. I was going by faith, and God would supply everything. Again, I thought of Abraham, who, "by faith ... when he was called, obeyed by going out to a place which he was to receive for an inheritance; and he went out, not knowing where he was going." (Hebrews 11:8)

As the train edged northward, I began to weep. In fact, my crying became so intense, other passengers expressed concern. They didn't understand that I was looking out the window at the villages passing by. There were so many people in those little places who needed God's message. My heart was breaking. I sobbed continuously for the perishing multitudes. I was also praying constantly. In spite of my tears, I felt God right next to me on the rocking, grinding train.

I arrived in Sambalpur, Orissa State, at midnight. There was a total blackout in the city due to a power outage. Everyone slept. There was no candle nor faint bed-light. I was fearful in the body, but strong in the spirit. I sang to myself:

> When darkness seems to hide His Face,
> I rest on His unchanging grace ...
> On Christ the solid rock I stand,
> All other ground is sinking sand ...

NEITHER FOOD NOR SHELTER

Though I could not communicate, somehow I got a rickshaw man to peddle me to a distant church. There was no one there to help. I walked off into the darkness. I had neither food nor shelter. I sagged, exhausted, onto a veranda and slept soundly.

The next morning, I started into the streets, on the King's business for which I had come. I distributed tracts, studying the faces of people who took them. Hopelessness was etched deep in their countenances. Again, I started to weep.

At last, I saw a face I knew, an acquaintance of my father, and a solid Christian. While his family was not able to accommodate me, I was able to leave some of my gear at his house. Life in Orissa was stark and difficult, but I reminded myself I was not there on a holiday, but a mission. I slept on trains, platforms, roads and streets. Often, the trees were the roof over my head.

Fifteen days had passed, and I only had 15 more before the deadline I had agreed to with my father. In two weeks, I had to win an Orissa person to Christ, if I wanted dad's blessing. Spurred by the driving calendar, I preached in the streets. One day, a crowd gathered. I spotted a young rickshaw man, listening intently. He was muscular from his ox-like work. I watched him as he put his rickshaw aside, and drew near to listen.

The crowd dispersed, but the brawny man approached me. "I've heard about you," he said. "I want to receive your Jesus! My name is Pani. Would you come to my house?"

The rugged man looked like a gang leader to me. My soul was fearful, but my spirit was courageous, so I walked in the spirit. I followed the young man through narrow, winding paths deep into the backstreets of the town. By now it was dark. The young man spoke no more. I followed, assured of the Presence of Jesus.

'HOW CAN HE BE MY FRIEND?'

Finally, we arrived at a shack, which measured no more than six-by-eight feet. Four or five children slept on the floor. I saw Pani's wife inside also. In the custom, she touched my feet and welcomed me inside. As we sat on the hard floor, Pani barraged me with questions. He was very hungry spiritually. He interpreted my message to his wife in their language.

"How can I come to this Jesus?" he asked. "You seem to talk of God as though you know Him intimately. But if He is a God, how can He be my friend?"

"Yes, He is God," I replied, "your God and my God, too. He is the universal God, Lord of creation."

Pani stared back, trying to absorb the words. Then he translated them to his wife. Turning back to me, he asked,

"How can I get in touch with this God?"

I gave Pani the Gospel. I spoke to him of the life-story of Jesus. As I spoke of the cross and crucifixion of Jesus, Pani's wife began to weep. Before my eyes, I saw the reality of Romans 1:16, which says the Gospel is the "power of God for salvation to everyone who believes ..."

Pani and his family were going through rough times, with many problems. They were most unhappy. The words I spoke gave them hope for this present life and the one to come. They began to grasp the fact that Jesus Christ is sufficient for all their personal problems, family concerns and spiritual well-being.

Pani and his wife were serious. "I've spoken to gods and told them about our need for food, clothing and safety, but do they hear? Do they even have ears?"

"Talk to Jesus as you would a friend," I responded. "Believe that He will arrive when you call. He will hear, take note and answer you."

'WHAT DO WE DO?'

I continued to talk to them for several hours. Finally, with the agreement of his wife, Pani asked, "What do we do to be saved?"

I opened the Bible to Acts 2:37-42, which says,

> Now when they heard this, they were pierced to the heart, and said to Peter and the rest of the apostles, "Brethren, what shall we do?" And Peter said to them, "Repent, and let each of you be baptized in the name of Jesus Christ for the forgiveness of your sins; and you shall receive the gift of the Holy Spirit. For the promise is for you and your children, and for all who are far off, as many as the Lord our God shall call to Himself."

And with many other words he solemnly testified and kept on exhorting them, saying, "Be saved from this perverse generation!" So then, those who had received his word were baptized; and there were added that day about three thousand souls.

I explained this Scripture to Pani and his wife. At the end, they were more than ready, and this Hindu man and his wife both accepted Christ.

I knew the call to Orissa which was so strong in my heart would now be confirmed in me father's heart. The burden which had weighted me down at the start of the day was now lifted. I immediately sent a message to my dad, telling of Pani's conversion. I asked my father to come and baptize Pani and his wife. Dad arrived speedily, and questioned Pani and his wife thoroughly. Father was satisfied, and baptized them on the 25th day of my arrival in Orissa.

HOUSE CHURCH LAUNCHED

I visited Pani's little box-like shack daily, feeding him and is wife God's Word. We also started a house church in the little tin structure. Pani knew three languages, so he interpreted. It helped me spread the Gospel. Pani's problems took wings as he continued believing, and the peace of God ruled in the hearts of Pani and his wife. "Poverty" no longer described their home. Christ became its head, and He cared for them in every respect. He transformed Pani from a sinner to a servant, helping me translate and assisting in other areas of ministry. In fact, Pani and his family began to prosper financially, and were even able to move into a larger house. They lived in a state of gratitude to God.

My dad was more than convinced of my call to Orissa. The ministry there marked the beginning of my mission to the untold and unreached. Since then, I have seen as many as one million people attend our evangelistic crusades at a time, yet I always think of the small start in the tiny tin house of Pani and his wife.

He and I traveled extensively, conducting crusades in villages. We did not know how much God had in store for us. We saw the devil defeated and Christ triumphant. Many villagers who had been heathen made Him the supreme Lord of their lives. We also experienced persecutions as we moved through Orissa State. But it was worth the cost as we saw gang leaders and prostitutes turn to Christ, along with many others.

Before, they all had been in the category of "unreached peoples." But now they had been touched by the Lord Himself.

LEFT FOR DEAD
K.A. PAUL OF INDIA

Chapter 7--A Cow-Shed Resting Place

I had several strange encounters with snakes in Orissa which seemed to symbolize my ongoing battle with the ancient serpent–Satan himself.

One night I was sleeping in the open, as I did frequently. That morning, as I slowly came to consciousness and began to wipe the sleep from my eyes, I sensed a presence near me. Slowly, I turned my head. A cobra was asleep right next to me. I remained motionless a few minutes, holding my breath, even trying to still my heart. I agonized over what to do. Cobras have been known to out-run human beings. Still, I knew my only escape would be to dart away. Suddenly, I bolted. Miraculously, the drowsy snake did not pursue me.

DANGERS FROM COBRAS

Another time, I stepped on the tail of a cobra. Again, I ran as fast as I could, and the dangerous animal did not follow. On yet another occasion, I came face to face with a cobra. Its hood was extended–a sign of imminent attack. Cobras are somewhat lethargic in the daytime, and prefer the night. The sun was up and so was my adrenalin. Again, I dashed away, before the languid beast could strike.

Everything in nature is a type of spiritual reality. I was being taught that I must be constantly alert to the serpent, the devil. Like the cobras, he prefers the darkness for his deadly work. In Christ, we are able to walk, run and soar. Sometimes, that means we are able to flee the devil before he can sink in his fangs. But I was also being rooted with the understanding that as long as the man or woman of God under the Lordship of Christ, pursuing His will, the enemy cannot destroy such a person.

But it wasn't just cobras that were a threat in Orissa. It was the lifestyle as well. My needs were few. All I had was a small bag I carried along with me. At night, it served as my pillow. Eventually, even the bag was stolen while I slept on a train station platform one night. I had nothing but God--and that was more than enough.

Though I must admit I did get physically hungry many times. At 19, I had a full appetite. Once, I was literally starving. It had been days since I had eaten. My stomach burned with hunger. I had only 15 pais, which is less than an American penny. I found a tea stall, and queued up anyway. I did not speak the language, and there were many people, so I had to wait a long time to get the attention of tea seller. He assumed I wanted to buy a cup, and quickly poured me tea, then moved to someone else, intending to collect from me later. I realized the tea cost 40 pais, and I didn't want to drink until I had told him I didn't have the full price.

BURNING PAIN

More people were lining up, so I approached him, and plopped the 15 pais in his hand. He said something in his language, which I assumed to be the fact that the tea cost 40 pais. Using signs, I indicated the 15 pais to be all I had. He took the tea away from me. Ashamed, I walked away slowly.

I was now in tears, crying over the burning pain in my hungry stomach. I walked slowly, my Bible in my hand. I saw a *tela*-a moving sales table--with lots of bananas. I still had almost no money and no language with which to negotiate. It was getting dark, and people were scooping up the bananas to take them home for an evening snack. I went to a side area, sat down, and gazed longingly at the bananas, crying to God.

As I saw the last customers leaving the *tela*, I walked over to the owner. Using signs, I tried to persuade him to give me a banana for my 15 pais. Indignant, he threw the money on the ground. I waited a few minutes, then approached him again. I noticed he had some spoiled bananas, and signed to him I would like to buy one for my 15 pais. He eyed me carefully. There was a faint, momentary God-given empathy in his eyes. "Yes," he nodded.

THE BLACK BANANA

I reached out and grabbed the black, moldy banana as fast as I could. The *tela* owner lent me his knife to cut away the spoiled part. As the last glimmer of twilight faded, I found a place to sit and eat my banana. I thanked God for it as I would have a meal of my mother's rice and shrimp curry. I wept as I ate, as the thought of the emotions and cravings of the last few days flooded my being. The banana was not enough to satisfy my total hunger, but it helped. I went to the public well, and pumped water with one hand into the other, from which I drank. Then I went out to share the Gospel. It was dangerous to walk in the streets and marketplaces after dark, but I wanted to show my appreciation for God's faithfulness.

As I write this story, my eyes fill with tears, as I think of the native missionaries working at this moment in the 10-40 Window countries. I pray they will have enough to eat for physical energy to preach the Gospel. They are truly dedicated to finish the task, but they depend on support which in many parts of the world seems meager, an average of $30 per month. With that amount, they feed their families, and are free to serve in fulltime ministry. I thank God for fellow Christians everywhere who care for these native missionaries, as well as widows and orphans.

A certain man had kept warning me not to preach about Jesus. Now he heard me declaring the Gospel. "You have not stopped all your preaching?" he screamed at me. Then he slapped me in the face. "I will kill you if you keep telling about this Jesus," he snarled. Nevertheless, I would preach, and he would stalk me. Finally, on one occasion, I sensed his presence and simply disappeared into the crowds. The man lost me, and never bothered me again.

The Orissa mission taught me that confrontation and antagonism are to be expected. It didn't surprise me when opponents would throw stones, or try to sow confusion in the crowds. Idol-worshippers are agitated when they hear the truth. Some, instead of yielding to the Gospel, deaden their consciences and convictions through violent behavior.

THE PAKNAM

It was in Orissa that I first understood the ferocity of the Paknam, who were to kidnap me years later in Calcutta--as described in Chapter 13. It seemed they would always be after my life. They would go to great cost and effort to stamp out the Gospel from India. Most Indians are non-violent. But this group was so bitter in their opposition, they would attack me openly, and even come to my home town to try to extinguish my witness.

The encounters with snakes and human beings who wanted my death made me grateful for the spiritual shelter I had in the Lord. I knew that was the only reason I continued alive. Yet since I had left home I had no resting place, physically. Cold weather was coming, robbers were constantly threatening me, so I decided to find a place to rent. I had little money, and to most people I was a stranger whom they might not want to trust living in their home. But now the weather was very cold, and I had to do something.

Christmas was drawing near, and God had a wonderful plan—as He did for Mary, Joseph and Baby Jesus. I discovered a cow-shed, and persuaded the owner to evict the animal and allow me to live in the six-by-ten shelter! There was no door, but I couldn't complain, since I only had to pay the equivalent of two dollars. When the cow left, unfortunately it didn't take its odor, but after much cleaning, I moved into my new "house."

I'm sure I was as grateful as an American who moves into a fancy new abode in a modern subdivision. At last I had a resting place, one of my own, with a roof over my head. That first night, I threw my body onto the sod, with only a thin sheet for cover. I had developed acute pain in my ribs and other bones from sleeping in the streets, and winced a little as my body settled onto the dirt floor. My parents had raised me in a comfortable home, with good food. Yet, after living in the streets, coming home to my cow-shed felt almost like arriving at our lovely house.

PEACE AND JOY

At 19, I was zealous and energetic in God's work. My passion was to reach the unreached by preaching in villages where the Gospel had never been announced. Despite my physical hardship, I had great peace and joy, knowing I was exactly where God wanted me. A person can endure almost anything if he or she is in the center of God's will. God was my constant Companion, Coverer and Counselor. Though my body ached, my spirit rejoiced, because I was fulfilling His plan for my life.

When I was running a business, I prospered, lived luxuriously and still gave away 50 percent of my income for missions. I loved the missionaries who lived in the jungles and among hill tribes. Now, as a missionary myself, I was facing a financial crisis. I had no money for even a single meal. No coffee, no tea, nothing. Yet I was never tempted to take a secular job. My only work was to reach souls. God's grace and provision proved sufficient in every situation.

The first Sunday service I conducted in Orissa was at Pani's house. The offering totaled 15 pais, less than one American cent. When I was in business, I would make as much as $200 a week, a huge amount in those days. But for six years, from 1983 to 1986, I hardly ever had a nice meal except when I visited my parents. Most of the time it seemed I would starve. There was no church or support group to which I could turn. God would move on individuals to help with a few rupees.

MUD FLOOR

So, each night in my cow-shed resting place, I slept on the mud floor, which was usually damp. I had no blanket, and hardly a meal a day. Once, the owner of the cow-shed asked me about a cot, bedding and other necessities. "It's all coming," I said, by faith. Then the landlord asked me for rent. "It's coming," I replied again. In two months, he asked me again. He was a post master, and assumed there had been a delay in the mail which had slowed the arrival of my rent.

Most Indians believe native evangelists are sponsored by Americans. A few are, but the majority serve under great financial stress and strain, without a sponsor. They have a call, a message and a burden for the lost, so they jog from village to village. There are many valiant servants of God, known only to Him, serving in India and other countries of the 10-40 Window. Day by day, they fight the spiritual foe and the physical opponents, ranging from starvation to the Paknam. No one writes of them, for they are unknown. But their names on the Heart of the Father, and they are among the heroes of His Kingdom.

Often I wondered why God permitted me so many

difficulties, especially in Orissa, where I was–and remain–certain He called me. I thank Him now that I can identify with His ministers who serve at the edge of poverty. There is distorted teaching in the West that God makes people rich when they turn to Him. The good in this doctrine is that it holds forth the truth that God desires the blessing of His children. But that blessing flows with a personal lifestyle of submission to Biblical principles regarding money. There are many individual believers in developing nations who adhere to Biblical guidelines in their own lives, but live in the context of the nation, a corporate system where God's principles are violated daily. If such faithful believers are not wealthy, it is not their fault, nor is it God's. The blame must lie with evil behind corporate financial structures under which people live in national systems.

ALLOWED TO STAY

In the midst of their hardship, such servants of God find His grace sufficient, that God supplies for the work He calls us to do. I experienced that. Even though I could not pay rent in my cow-shed home for two months, miraculously, I was not cast out.

I usually ministered to people on the street and those en route to their work places. Once I happened to meet Kutty, a brother from Kerala State, in the deep south of India. He was an officer in a food services corporation. He invited me to his home, where I told him of my call to Orissa. He was pleased to hear my story, and gave me a delicious meal. In fact, it was the first time since stepping into full time ministry I had dined so well.

The following morning, I was praying earnestly for my house note to be paid. There was a knock at the door. It was Kutty. He brought me breakfast. While I gobbled it down, Kutty asked where I lived. "This cow shed is my home," I replied, to his shock. Kutty then promised to visit me that evening with his wife.

We had a wonderful visit that evening, discussing many things. Suddenly his wife asked, "Where is your bed?"

I could only point to the floor.

Then Kutty and his wife gave me 120-rupees for a cot, and then left. It was the exact amount I needed for the two months' rent. I began to wonder how I could buy a cot without paying rent, and how I could use cot-money for rent. Then there was another knock at the door. Kutty had returned. "You can use the money any way you like," he said, then left again. My prayer had been answered before I could speak it!

I paid my landlord, and he asked, "Did the postman come?"

"Yes," I responded, "the man came."

Kutty was God's "postman." In fact, he was the Lord's messenger to me in other ways. When he discovered that I had chosen not to spend the money on a cot, he and another donor brought me a bed.

At last, my cow-shed resting place was furnished with all I needed.

LEFT FOR DEAD
K.A. PAUL OF INDIA

Chapter 8--Conversion Leads To Torture

Budan was a bubbly but sophisticated government official who wanted to know God's plan for his life. We would talk, and out of his spiritual hunger he would ply me with questions. He wanted to confirm that Jesus Christ is the only way to the Father, and why he should deny other gods.

"You're not denying a 'god,'" I answered. "These things are just dumb idols. They don't respond to your requests--good or bad."

MORE QUESTIONS

Budan thought about this a few days. Then he came back with more questions: "Does Jesus really forgive sins? If He does, then why? How can I get forgiveness?"

"There is only one living God, and the others are but illusions," I told Budan. "The real God wants fellowship with us. Jesus is not a killer nor destroyer; He doesn't want to hurt people, or scare us."

Budan listened intently, taking in the words.

"In fact," I continued, "He begins by saying, 'fear not.' Jesus doesn't demand sacrifices; He sacrificed Himself for us. He took our sins on Himself, and bore the punishment, so only He can forgive us."

Budan had never heard of such a God.

"If you ask Him, He will forgive your sins and lift the curses off you," I said. "He asks nothing of you materially, but seeks your heart. He will flood you with His love."

Budan and I visited many more times. Finally, he accepted Christ as His Savior. This man of high position and education and reputation in Orissa turned to the Lord. Budan and I became good friends. We both learned how costly salvation is. Budan had to forsake the "gods" of his forefathers. For me, the cost was torture.

The Paknam found out about Budan's conversion. They knew that because of Budan's position and the respect with which he was held, his whole village might turn to Christ. The leader of the Paknam in that area called together his henchmen. Their assignment was to kill me as I traveled about. If they failed, they risked being killed themselves. There were 17 in the death squad assigned to murder me. They divided into one team of 10 and another of seven. There were only two roads in and out of town. I would leave by one and return by the other. But now both roads were guarded by the Paknam.

JUNGLE ENCOUNTER

After finishing a Bible study with Budan, I motored off on a small mo-ped. After riding sometime, almost into the jungles, I encountered a group of young men standing side by side on the road, blocking my travel. Someone grabbed my scooter and drove away with it. The other men grabbed me and dragged me into the jungle. They beat me to their satisfaction.

"Why are you converting people to Christianity?" they screamed at me. "Didn't we warn you to leave this place and stop your work here?"

They didn't wait for me to answer, but kept pounding me.

"These Christians receive tons of cash from foreigners for each conversion, and that's why they don't stop making converts," one of the Paknam yelled.

This infuriated the men even more, and they tore my

clothes as they beat me. Finally, they stopped and began speaking with one another about what they should do to me next.

One of the Paknam turned to me and snarled, "let your God now come and save you from our hands!"

"Today is your last day," another one spat at me, "so you will not be spreading your religion any more. We are going to bury you in minutes, in this very jungle!"

"I am not receiving money for conversions," I said. "I'm simply sharing my faith, telling people that Christ died to forgive our sins."

JABBED WITH QUESTIONS

The Paknam now jabbed with questions: "Why do you condemn other gods? What do you mean to say that only Christians go to Heaven? Are all the rest of people lost?"

Their collective temper flared. We were all trying to speak in our broken English since we didn't speak each other's languages. This added to the confusion and frustration, especially as they tried to draw a comparison between their false gods and Jesus.

"Let's tie him to a tree and burn him up," one of them suggested.

"That's too complicated," said another.

"Let's bury him alive, and that will teach all Christians a good lesson not to preach any more."

I was praying hard. Suddenly, I had a deep assurance that I would be able to run away, despite the fact blood was oozing from every part of my body and was weak from the beatings. It was by the mercy of God that I was still breathing after such savage treatment. Yet inside, I could hear the words, "Run! Run! Run!" The group moved a few yards away in a huddle. They were plotting how best to execute me and prove to their leader

I was really dead.

While they were planning, I leapt to my feet. I had been a fast racer in college, and now my old skill returned, in spite of my wounds. I still had Heaven on my side, and God's grace, which my enemies did not have. God had prepared me from my mother's womb to be a runner for this very moment, I thought. Deeper into the jungle I ran, hopping over bushes, darting around prickly growths. The Paknam were pursuing. I could hear their voices. Finally, though, I came to the main road.

ESCAPE

God goes before us, knowing when we sit down and rise up, says the Psalmist. He certainly went before me that day, and arranged my escape. When I got to the main road, I spotted a truck passing by. I cast my self in front of the vehicle, not fearing it would run over me. I shouted praise to God as the truck stopped. The Sikh driver jerked me in. Just then the Paknam came running up, but the driver cursed them and told them to get out of the way. He assumed they were highway bandits.

By God's mercy, I arrived home alive. On entering the cow-shed, I locked the door, and began praising and worshipping God. I knew my situation was still dangerous. Perhaps the Paknam had tracked me to my cow-shed. Or, maybe they had simply inquired of someone where the young preacher lives.

It was the Paknam who beat me seven times. Once, they bashed me so severely they left me for dead. Yet I am alive. Life and death are from Above. Again I understood that one cannot die until God's plans for that life are fulfilled.

But I came to live in a tense, uneasy relationship with the Paknam. I could not stop preaching the Gospel, and they would not cease trying to beat and torture and kill me. They stalked me, digging into my activities. They wanted to know how many people were turning to Christ, how many people were being baptized, how many villages hearing the Gospel.

Often, they would go before me into a village and warn and instigate leaders to thrash me and send me away. Often I had to flee villages even before I started preaching. Nevertheless, I was privileged to plant and pastor five churches in 1984 and 1985. The churches were far apart, and all needed by attention. On Sundays, I was busy with the churches until midnight. Then, during the week, I visited each church every other day. Many of the people were illiterate, and I had to feed them the Word of God without them being able to read the Bible.

NO OTHER PLACE

Though it was hard work, I wouldn't have swapped places with any other leader. Since there was neither post nor telephone, I had to reach them personally. The newly saved people were growing in the Lord. They were spiritually hungry, and always had new questions. Yet doctrine had to be introduced slowly. This included teachings about tithing. So, offerings were meager. I didn't have enough to repair my bike nor even to buy soap to wash my clothes.

Our little church experienced its privations as well. There was no seating, no Bibles, no hymn books, no musical instruments. We did have our voices and hands, so we praised God with song and shout, and clapped our adoration of Him. Our hearts were zealous for the Lord. The members began experiencing persecution for their faith, and I spent much time praying with them. It was important to build them up, and encourage them to keep walking, despite the tribulations.

No matter how great or lowly a person in the world's esteem, he or she needs God to satisfy the innermost need. One day, while distributing tracts, an attorney stopped me and took me to his home. He closed the door, making sure no one could hear, and asked me serious questions about Jesus. "How can Jesus be the only God?" he inquired.

As I began my reply, he became angry, because he couldn't refute what I was saying. The truth burned as it touched his soul, as an antiseptic washing an open wound. Suddenly he struck me. The blow was so strong, my jaw shook and blood flowed. "Either you prove to me today, logically, that Jesus Christ is God, or I will kill you on the spot!" he snarled.

DARKNESS BRINGS TEARS

Though my jaw hurt, I rejoiced because he was inviting me to continue to talk about Jesus. I began weeping, not from my pain, but because of his darkness. "Hear me with an open heart," I pled, through the tears and blood. I then told him of my father's salvation, and how Jesus had broken through the barriers of Hinduism, high caste, cruelty, saved him, healed him and transformed him. I told the lawyer about my dad's quest in the Hindu temples, and the futility of his search in those places. I spoke of my father's decision to murder his family and commit suicide, and how the Lord had rescued us all.

The attorney gazed at me with piercing eyes, his mind seeming to focus on every syllable coming from my mouth. "How can Jesus be greater than Krishna, who I am following?" he asked.

"Jesus is holy in every respect," I replied. "His birth is holy, His life is holy, His resurrection is holy, His ascension is holy. As holy God, He washes His people in His holy Blood and takes them finally to Heaven."

I spoke to the attorney like this for what seemed to be hours. At last, he interrupted me.

"Do you think Krishna is not holy because he has thousands of girl friends?" the lawyer asked.

"It is not my desire to criticize religions, but one thing I know is that God is a holy Being," I responded. "He cannot have unholy relationships."

One never knows what God will use to break through a resistant heart. But for this attorney, the awesomeness of God's holiness seemed to be the key. At last he was convinced, and received Christ as his Savior. He even repented for hitting me and asked me to pray for him right away.

It was worth the suffering, the shedding of a little blood, the hours of tension and explanation of God's Word. When we finished, he took me to a nearby restaurant and fed me. We both feasted over his salvation, joining the celebration of the angels in Heaven over this lost soul who had found his Savior.

LEFT FOR DEAD
K.A. PAUL OF INDIA

Chapter 9--Marriage

Often, our destiny touches us with the faint glance of a feather, and we do not know we are in its presence.

On December 25, 1985, at 4 a.m., after an eight-hour service I conducted, several people responded to the Gospel. Though I did not know, several were my future in-laws. Later that morning, we went to a place where there was water. In the family that had received Christ was a lovely young daughter. As I lowered the young woman into the waters, I had no idea that someday she would be my wife. In those years, I wasn't thinking of marriage at all. Yet as I laid hands on her in the baptism service, I was touching my destiny and she was in the presence of hers.

BIBLICAL NAMES

Each member of the family took a Biblical name. The father became Abraham, the mother Sarah and the daughter who would become my wife, Mary.

I call June 14, 1986, my "good day," because that was the date of our wedding. We were married in my home town, in the church led by my dad. Pastor Deva Sahayami, president of an organization with hundreds of churches in India, solemnized our wedding and preached a great sermon. Hundreds of people shared the day with us, and heard the pastor encourage us to share the totality of life and ministry.

An Indian wedding is celebrated in many places. Festivals and feastings were conducted in the homes of aunts and uncles and friends. We enjoyed ourselves everywhere we went. I learned why Americans speak of a "shower" when they refer to a party for brides and grooms. Wherever we went, people showered us with gifts, special food and rich love. Those happy memories will remain with us always. Our joy know no bounds. I would that all marriages were as happy as ours. Our happiness did not depend on dowry, wealth and jewelry.

In fact, it's a custom in India for the bride to bring much wealth into the marriage, or else the relationship might not last. Our Christian marriage was not based on earthly treasures, but on our common faith in Jesus Christ. In the Bible, the men gave gifts to the women. We followed the Biblical custom rather than that of the culture of our country. Christ was our chief Guest. Once I had read in the newspaper about three young women committing suicide because they did not ave a sufficient dowry to bring into a marriage. They were harassed by in-laws, and so they committed suicide. Because we had Jesus, we needed nothing else. He was the "Dowry" we brought into the marriage and through Whom we blessed one another.

BACK TO ORISSA

After our wedding, Mary and I returned to live in Orissa. We stayed there two years, from 1986-1988. That state is dotted with hundreds of jungle villages, isolated places which are among the unreached areas of the world. My call is to the unreached, so Mary and I sought to go where the Gospel had not been preached and base there. In one place we found three Christian families. The metal factory for which the men worked had transferred them there. We were able to establish house churches in their homes and these became centers for the spread of the Gospel into the whole region.

Jesus said that "this gospel of the kingdom will be preached in all the world as a witness to all the nations, and then the end will come." (Matthew 24:14) "World," in the New

Testament Greek, refers specifically to inhabited places. To think of Orissa is to be drawn to the scope of God's plan. Jesus will not return until His Word has been preached in all the inhabited world!

God did not forget Mary and me in our jungle home. We had been married but a few weeks, with no money nor property. We had a few clothes and our Bibles. We traveled throughout the region, realizing that we married for Christ and the church. We saw ourselves as co-travelers for our Lord and His Kingdom. Of course Christ Himself traveled a great deal. So Mary and I felt close to the Lord as journeyed from place to place in Orissa.

AMBUSH

Once Mary and I had traveled for 12 long hours on an over-crowded train. It was being brought to a halt every few minutes. Even deep in the jungle it would linger for 20 minutes at a time at lonely stations. After one long stop, the train began chugging again. Suddenly, well into the trip, someone pulled the emergency stop chain. No one knew that a number of thieves had jumped on the train. Next the lights went off. It was night, and very dark in the thick jungle. In the darkness, the thieves scampered through and scooped up jewelry, luggage and other belongings.

When I realized what was happening, I jumped up. My suitcase was gone. It contained all we had: our valuable papers, wedding certificate, clothing. We had lost everything except the clothes we wore. I told Mary. "Let us bind the powers of darkness," she said. We held hands and prayed in front of all the passengers. We understood the meaning of "two are better than one." We presented our case to the Almighty.

Specifically, we stood on Matthew 18:18, believing that whatever we bind on earth shall be bound in Heaven. "Now, we agree that the suitcase which was stolen must be found," I prayed. "Right now, whoever the man is who is carrying our suitcase, let him be caught by somebody. We release the ministering angels to do whatever is needful." When I stopped praying, it was 4 a.m.

Meanwhile, a forest guard officer was routinely going through his duties, which included protecting that part of the jungle bordering the train track. At exactly 4 a.m. he saw a young man dragging a heavy suitcase. "That is a pretty nice suitcase," the guard said. "Where are you going with it so early in the morning?"

The thief could not answer, so the officer became suspicious and took the man into custody. The guard compelled him to drag the heavy bag to the station, where someone recognized him as one of the thieves. The villagers gave the man a severe beating, and tied him to a tree.

SUITCASE RECOVERED

Meanwhile, I was leading a worship service, which concluded about 1 p.m. There was neither train nor bus transportation available to go on to the village, so I hitched a ride with a truck, leaving my wife with friends.

When we arrived at our destination, we gave our complaint to the railroad officials. They had already received a phone call that a suitcase had been found. I was asked to describe my bag. When they saw it fit the description of the one found, an official said, "it is your luck." He went on to explain that all the thieves dispersed to various villages. The only piece of property recovered was our suitcase!

I told the official I wanted to withdraw my complaint. I asked to be taken to the thief. When I was brought to him, he was bleeding and in great pain. He happened to be from one of the villages to which we had moved to pioneer a church and reached the area's unevangelized people. In fact, the thief recognized me because he and his gang had been angry with me for preaching against stealing, killing and other criminal acts. They also knew a previous gang leader had accepted Christ through our ministry, and so the whole gang led by the bleeding man I now saw harnessed to the tree had targeted me.

I am continually wonder-struck at God's love for sinners. He would rather save the worst than destroy them. So I spoke to the thief about God's love and salvation. He seemed to understand. I told him that if he were willing to change his life and turn to Jesus, I would do all I could to convince the police department and avert prison. I wept for him, and he began weeping as well.

"I have been a thief from childhood," he said.

As he talked, I discovered he was from my area, and knew many people I know. There was a common bond between us.

"Why don't you work and support your family rather than robbing people?" I asked him.

SPARING THE THIEF

Meanwhile, the villagers were upset. They were waiting for me to register my complaint officially, and then see the thief get his punishment. Murmurings started in the mob. "Let's take things into our own hands," someone suggested. "Let's kill him on the spot! He's a gangleader whose gang has murdered many people! We don't need the police. We'll take justice into our own hands!"

Because the mob was so infuriated, I knew he wouldn't be safe at the station. I told the officers that I would take the man with me. I felt this is what the love of Christ would compel me to do.

"Don't be foolish," a member of the crowd said, when the people received word of my intention. "That thief will kill you on the way," they warned. We had spent the entire day on the matter, and now darkness was approaching again. The night seemed to deepen as more and more villagers came to see this notorious thief. It gave them great pleasure to see him tied up. But now they were growing restless. Anger was slowly brewing against me as well, for extending forgiveness to the thief. So I turned and began preaching the Gospel to the mob.

"Please, give me your attention," I cried. "I know of a great thief in my home town. No one was able to control him. He excelled at robbery, and was very cruel. No one could change him--except the living God. Today that man who was a thief is now a servant of God. Christ can change human nature unto divine nature. God gives but does not rob. When somebody turns to God in repentance, that person receives God's nature. People without God can commit any sin without being disturbed. But now I have given this thief the truth about God."

'WE HAVE ALL SINNED'

The crowd continued to listen. "When Christ died for sinners, a thief was on a cross next to Him. This thief repented in his dying moments, and called on Jesus to forgive him. Jesus, Who is more than happy to forgive, told him, 'this day you will be with Me in Paradise.' What the law cannot do, God can do. The law only condemns and punishes. But Christ has the power to forgive sins if one repents. We have all sinned, and not just this thief."

I preached until late in the night, but the people remained, listening. I began to realize they respected my arguments. I said a prayer of forgiveness for them all, believing the Holy Spirit was convicting them. Gradually, they withdrew. No one was left to cast a stone at the thief who had stolen my suitcase. Finally, when I would not post a complaint, the official left as well.

Now I was alone with the thief, prayed with him, and he accepted Jesus. We all returned to the village we shared. I watched the man over time as he gave up crime and took a job. His family, which almost lost him that night, could now look on him with respect.

But is wasn't just thieves Mary and I had to deal with on our jungle journeys: there were wild animals as well. Usually, I had to walk, though occasionally a bicycle was available. The forests were thick and dark; here and there were steep bluffs and ruddy hills to climb. It was common to hear the roaring of tigers and howling of other wild animals as we made our way through the Orissa jungles. But always, we were conscious of God's Presence.

BRUSH WITH DEATH

Once I was travelling with a friend, Braja Mohan, and others, to an interior village, far from a city or town. My friends climbed a hill carrying their bicycles. I, however, couldn't climb the hill–even without a bicycle on my back. I stumbled and rolled down the dusty slope. Again, God saved me. Just as I was about to tumble over the edge and a drop of several hundred feet, I was able to snag a branch. Once again, I knew I would not die until my mission is fulfilled.

In such moments, I refuse to think I am "close" to death. After all, life is as close as death. This is one of the revelations that has sustained me under torture. My life comes from Above, and cannot be tampered with until the Lord above declares my task finished. Jesus Himself did not die "before time," but "on time." The Bible says He came in the "fullness of time." That is, when chronos-time–the passing of the calendar–reached the right moment, then came the kairos-time, the "fullness" of time. Every day is precious to us, but every step is God's concern. The steps of a righteous man are ordered by the Lord. K.A. Paul, in himself is not naturally a righteous man. But Jesus is perfectly righteous, and Jesus indwells me. He is my life.

Therefore, because Christ is in me and I am in Christ, I am a righteous man, and therefore my steps are ordered by the Lord. These are promises I live and travel by–and they are for all committed followers of the Lord Jesus Christ.

These promises have carried me through many situation, like one that occurred in Fall, 1992. I was traveling with Indian and Canadian friends into the jungles. We drove in two cars. After 20 hours of rugged riding, we reached a remote village. Just then one of the cars began giving trouble. There is no phone system in the deep Indian jungles, no motels or inns or friendly mechanics, no service stations. There is, however, plenty of danger. We had no choice but to try to eke out some more miles from the car. Miraculously, we pastors, who lacked mechanical skills, were able to coax the car to run. In fact, it chugged along until we reached the next village, and then stopped again.

NO '911' BUT '91:1'

Darkness had come to the jungle, and the deep growth shrouded the night with a deeper grimness than usual. We didn't have "911," but we did have Psalm 91:1! We were under the foreboding shadows of the jungle, but that Psalm told us we also were under a greater Shadow–the protective covering of the Most High.

We were on constant alert for cobras and tigers. Again, we struggled with the car. Again, God gave pastors mechanical skills we don't normally possess. After 51 hours of stop and go driving, we arrived at the village which had been our destination. The people were excited to see the white-skinned Canadians. They danced and praised God according to their tribal tradition. The people invited us into their homes.

Paul James, leader of the village churches, translated our message into the local dialect. Two years later, Paul would be cut into pieces for preaching the Gospel. Several people that night, however, accepted Christ, and we baptized them. It gave us all great joy to see tribal people, most illiterate, some not even clothed, yet still grasping the love of God.

And though the jungles were teeming with tigers, we saw none. We had prayed to be protected from the beasts, and that night, no tigers came into the village. They didn't even roar, and we all rested well.

Eventually, Mary and I settled in Thiruballi, where I pioneered and pastored a church. Many times in that period I saw tigers. Once while travelling about twilight, an enormous tiger was blocking the road ahead, fast asleep. We stopped our vehicle and waited what seemed hours for the majestic animal to awaken and clear our path. There's an old saying in America: "It's better to let sleeping dogs lie." Believe me, it's even better to let sleeping tigers lie.

TIGER STIRRED

Meanwhile another vehicle arrived from the other direction. A driver began honking a horn and flashing lights at the tiger. I wondered which set of passengers the tiger would eat first. Now the tiger stirred, and grew upset at the blaring horn and flashing light. Just as I thought the tiger would pounce on one of the vehicles, it turned and walked quietly into the jungle.

Again and again, God would assure me of His protective care in the dangerous places we traveled. Once, I almost bumped into a sleeping bear. Something alerted me before the collision, and I peddled my bicycle as fast as possible in the other direction. Another night I was sleeping outside our house in the cool breeze, while Mary was away, visiting her mother. The tin shed which was our abode was unbearably hot during the summer. In fact, many people would sleep outside.

A tiger wandered into the village. People scampered into

their homes, but I slept soundly, even though the animal--who would kill a person in the next village--passed near the place where I was sleeping. "He gives His beloved sleep," says Psalm 127:2, and I snoozed without interruption, though the hungry tiger was sniffing and pawing nearby.

Yet another time, my partner, Abraham, and I were returning through a jungle thicket after conducting a Gospel crusade. We were warned not to risk such a trip at night. The people told us it was dangerous to take the journey in the daytime, and deadly at night. There were no roads, just narrow winding paths. A ferocious bear was one of the residents along this route, and had recently killed a man, as had a tiger. In fact, the brother of the young man killed by the tiger had gone into the jungle to shoot the animal. The man missed his shot, and the tiger wounded him.

MOVING DANGEROUSLY

I have to admit that in those days I sometimes made foolish decisions I mistook for boldness. Getting through was my aim rather than safety and security. I was also sure of Divine protection. But God also had to teach me the balance of wisdom, common sense and discretion so I could discern when I was moving dangerously in a cocky human spirit and not His Holy Spirit. My life then was like a vehicle without brakes. All I wanted to do was go, work and preach. I needed God's teaching about balance. Without it, we get beyond His chosen place for us. When we do that, we get outside His covering and anointing. This is why Jesus said He did nothing He didn't first see the Father doing. One has to listen and watch for God's signal before moving out.

This is crucial for every believer. However, when one lives constantly at the edge of crisis, hearing God becomes a matter--literally--of life and death. The most important issue for daily living, then, is the continual communion with the Father through which His child hears God's Voice.

LEFT FOR DEAD
K.A. PAUL OF INDIA

Chapter 10--Living At The Edge

My experience is typical of many, if not most, indigenous missionaries, evangelists, pastors and church leaders ministering in the world's most unreached areas. We live constantly at the edge of crisis. We could say with the Apostle Paul:

> I have been on frequent journeys, in dangers from rivers, dangers from robbers, dangers from my countrymen, dangers from the Gentiles, dangers in the city, dangers in the wilderness, dangers on the sea, dangers among false brethren; I have been in labor and hardship, through many sleepless nights, in hunger and thirst, often without food, in cold and exposure. (2 Corinthians 11:26-27)

Such a lifestyle mandates hearing God precisely for every step. Again, consider Paul. There were times when God blocked him from going certain places. (See, for example, Acts 16:7.) But how did Paul and the other apostles hear the Lord? What lifestyle did they pursue that sharpened their spiritual hearing?

The closer you are to God in personal communion, the clearer you understand His plan for your life. The gap between a person and God may be the reason one does not know His will nor have strength to overcome the evil one. We ought to be occupied more with the vastness of God than the vastness of our work.

Jesus said that we must abide in Him, for apart from Him, we can do nothing. (John 15:4-5) Many of us are willing to have a coffee break with Jesus, but abiding means much more than a brief visit. In the original Greek, "abide" means to dwell, to continue. A visitor we allow at our table for a sip of tea or coffee does not abide. I abide with my wife. We share destiny, as well as the issues of daily life. If I suffer, she suffers, and vice-versa. If one prospers, we both prosper.

My travel schedule causes me to be away from home often and for extended periods. But it makes me feel all the more how much I desire fellowship with my wife and children. It is hard for many of us to believe it, but our Father allows Himself to desire fellowship with us. By definition, God is all-sufficient. The only need He has is that which He permits Himself to experience. It should show us all how much we are valued that the God Who is above every need lets Himself need us!

MORE INTIMACY

As you linger in His Presence, He reveals more of His Mind to you. He grants you a greater revelation of Himself, His plans and purposes for your life. This is why the enemy works so hard to frustrate your time with the Father. Jesus says the thief comes to steal. (John 10:10) It's not just our lives the adversary wants to steal through death, but our *time* as well. God does not want us to walk in confusion, without guidance. But the demons find ground in our busy schedules, or our orientation toward work and performance. Using that opportunity, they blind us to the wonders of abiding in the Presence of God.

The ground is taken away immediately when we repent and make ourselves available to God as the number one priority of our lives. As we put away the distractions, which range from our work to the filling of time with futility–such as hours before a TV set–He increases us in spiritual power. As you wait before the Lord, He makes you spiritually robust. This is the revelation through Isaiah, who wrote:

> Yet those who wait for the LORD will gain new strength; they will mount up with wings like eagles, they will run and not get tired, they will walk and not become weary. (Isaiah 40:31)

As I noted in a previous chapter, from the time of my parents' conversion to Christ, our household pursued commitment without reservation. As a three-year old lad, I was introduced into our family pattern of fasting every Saturday. I hated it. I scampered here and there, looking for bits and morsels of food, robbing from anybody available. I would hoard little bits of food and eat secretly.

NOT LEGALISM

Some might accuse my parents of legalism. But if so, it would only be because the accusers didn't understand where my father and mother had walked. They had been enemies of Christ and His Church. Others had prayed with fasting for my parents, and they knew this is what God used to bring them to the crises that opened them to Christ. In fact, a godly pastor and his whole congregation of four other believers had prayed 18 hours a day for the conversion of the fanatic idol-worshippers who were my parents. And those five believers fasted as they prayed.

My dad could not forget the torment he had undergone prior to knowing Jesus, and how he had come to the point of suicide for the whole family. My father remembered how a three-day fast had cleared spiritual vision so that salvation and healing became possible for him. A disease of three and one-half years came to a dead end. God used prayer with fasting to kill the disease. Prayer with fasting attracted God and my father received deliverance.

Does it sound offensive to say that "prayer with fasting attracted God"? It is not as strange as it sounds. Once, our daughter Grace asked me for a bicycle. I didn't pay much attention to her request. As a servant of God, I thought, I should use money to buy a bicycle for a village evangelist, not for my daughter. Grace, I figured, would get over her desire for the bicycle. But it was not to be. After all, her friends had bikes, and she didn't understand why she couldn't have one.

One day Grace came to me. "I will not eat food until you buy me a bicycle," she said. For the first time, I took her seriously. I realized having a bicycle was so important to my daughter, I gave her one. She was paying the cost for the bike to materialize.

God, of course, doesn't have to be convinced of our seriousness. He is omniscient, knowing the secrets of our hearts. But when we become so serious about what God has moved us to seek, then we are ready to receive. Fasting may be a sign to God of our readiness, but it is certainly to a sign to our own souls as to what we truly value and desire.

LEARN THE SECRET

The Western Church needs to learn the secret of prayer with fasting. In countries like China and India, where there is vicious persecution, Christ's people know how important it is. In emergencies and other crises, the automatic response of the believers is to go on an extended fast.

Is it possible that America is in such a time of need? Many have pondered why revival has not stirred broadly in America in recent times as it has in developing nations. Why is America turning away from God in her public institutions? We who come from outside the United States assume naively that America is a Christian nation, and that the American church walks in spiritual disciplines. It is a surprise to us when we discover that in spite of all the Bibles, Christian radio and television stations, church buildings, tape ministries, that there is not full-blown revival and commitment in America.

In the United States, it may be safe to say there is one preacher for about every 100 people. In the developing nations, we can travel into 10,000 villages and visit 10 million people without meeting just one Gospel preacher. So what is lacking in America?

If revival is to come to a country, it has to begin with the revival of individuals through repentance. Take, for example, the case of Nineveh. Jonah proclaimed God's Word to the Ninevites, and the following resulted:

> Then the people of Nineveh believed in God; and they called a fast and put on sackcloth from the greatest to the least of them. When the word reached the king of Nineveh, he arose from his throne, laid aside his robe from him, covered himself with sackcloth, and sat on the ashes. And he issued a proclamation and it said, "In Nineveh by the decree of the king and his nobles: do not let man, beast, herd, or flock taste a thing. Do not let them eat or drink water. But both man and beast must be covered with sackcloth; and let men call on God earnestly that each may turn from his wicked way and from the violence which is in his hands. Who knows, God may turn and relent, and withdraw His burning anger so that we shall not perish?" When God saw their deeds, that they turned from their wicked way, then God relented concerning the calamity which He had declared He would bring upon them. And He did not do it. (Jonah 3:5-10)

A sign of the seriousness of the Ninevites was in the fact they fasted. Every individual entered into this, with the ruler in the lead. Fasting implied their sincerity. It is a way of saying, "I would rather go without food until I hear the Voice of my Father." Fasting signifies that our desire is not some casual matter, but of even greater importance than food.

There are even those, like Jesus, who are led to fast as long as 40 days. This would seem an impossible period to fast. Yet if God leads one to fast 40 days, it is possible, because God knows the limits of the human body. Over such a long period, a person experiences the crucifixion of the flesh. The trials of hunger and weakness become as nothing when seen in the light of the miraculous results.

NOT A 'MUST'

A 40-day fast is not a must for all believers. It is for those God leads specifically to fast for such a long period. Persons should not feel guilty if, for medical reasons, or simply because they have no impulse from the Lord, they cannot fast 40 days. Again, God knows the limits of the human body, and will only lead those into such a long fast who can endure it. The point is that, for whatever period, the fast should be seen as an intensified time before God.

Every time I have fasted, it has been because God inspired, or called me to it, not because of a human impulse to manipulate God into a certain thing. At one point, God did call me into a 40-day fast. It was during this period I received from Him the clear vision for Gospel to the Unreached Millions. The seeding of our Bible schools for training indigenous missionaries to reach the unreached came during that long fast.

I began to realize that there are 27,000 ethnic groups comprising the world's 5.6 billion people. Pepsi and Coke have reached the villages, why not the Gospel? It was during the 40-day fast that I realized that instead of spending millions sending in English-speaking missionaries, why not train and equip the nationals? I weep daily for the unreached, as I realize that half the globe has yet to hear the Gospel.

The Church has enough money to evangelize the world. The need is for vision. One of the reasons the vision is not grasped is because of spiritual lethargy in the Church. This comes from not knowing the Mind of God, which is known, as we've said, through abiding communion with Him. Not waiting on Him leads to a lack of strategy, ignorance of God's plan. Noah was instructed by God how to build the Ark, Moses how to raise the tabernacle. So God wants to reveal to us how He wants His work done. He wants His servants to move by revelation, not reason. Revelation comes only as we spend the time before Him, and this often means fasting with prayer.

On the day I received the vision for Gospel to the Unreached Millions, I was in the midst of the fast, when I suddenly felt the unseen Presence. I felt like Moses must have felt when he was in the cleft of the rock, watching God pass by. As His manifest Presence drew near, I could discern His Mind. I knew the strategies of His Heart. When I saw the vision and plan, I stopped weeping. God strengthened me during the 40 days in His manifest Presence. In fact, as I saw His plan, I was invigorated.

800,000 DECISIONS

That was in the 1980s. Now, as I write, the 20th century is drawing to a close. But fresh in my mind is the fruit that came from the vision I received in that 40-day fast. Hot in my thoughts is a recent crusade sponsored by Gospel to the Unreached Millions. A great teacher, Bill Gothard--and others-- was with me as we ministered in a town in my native state, Andhra Pradesh. According to the crusade committee, more than 800,000 people accepted Christ, in the five-night event. Though some came from distant areas, all are being followed up as I write by workers trained by Gospel to the Unreached Millions, along with others. I likely would not have been in Kurnool without the vision that came during the fast, and I know the follow-up workers would not have been available for such a huge harvest.

But it's not just for endurance in persecution or for vision for ministry that we should pray with fasting. We need also to fast and pray regarding life's major personal decisions. As I considered marriage, for example, I knew I must marry exactly the right person. In an earlier chapter, I wrote of our marriage. But now I must add that fasting became an urgent necessity as I thought of marriage. I knew I had to have the mate God chose for me, one who could walk with me in the hard places, who would share the call, be able to endure the loneliness that comes from being married to an evangelist. God chose the very best for me in my dear wife, Mary. But I could only know His perfect will through spending time in His Presence through fasting and prayer.

ENTIRE NATIONS

My father, Barnabas, preaches about how prayer with fasting changes entire nations. There is much chaos in the nations today, and some in the Church are embracing the world's methods of violence, or putting their faith in political solutions to change the nations. Instead, followers of Christ must learn to fast and pray for the nations.

Consider, for example, Esther. A whole nation–the Jews– was going to be extinguished. Esther had to stand before the king, and show him the disastrous plot he had been drawn into. Before Esther undertook her dangerous mission, she sent word to her uncle, Mordechai:

"Go, assemble all the Jews who are found in Susa,

and fast for me; do not eat or drink for three days, night or day. I and my maidens also will fast in the same way. And thus I will go in to the king, which is not according to the law; and if I perish, I perish." (Esther 4:16)

As this entire group prayed with fasting, Esther went before the king, and the Jews were saved. A policy decision of state was altered. Had that national direction not been changed, the Messiah of Israel would not have come forth to save the world, because there would have been no Israel.

But it's not just the monumental things for which we can fast and pray to see a breakthrough. God's Eyes are on the most minute situations. Gospel to the Unreached Millions started an orphanage in Vishakapatnam, in Andhra Pradesh State, and other places in India. Once, the orphanage ran out of food, so the director prayed with fasting. When mealtime came, he instructed the staff to serve the children water first.

"Why should we serve water, when no food has been cooked?" one of the workers asked.

"Serve the water and seat the children before empty plates," the director instructed.

THE 'RAVEN'

The helpers obeyed. The director told everyone to bow for a prayer of blessing for the food. Suddenly, there was a knock at the gate, and when it was opened, a man was there, bearing food for the orphanage. In fact, it was especially good food, fit for the rich man's birthday. As Elijah had been fed by God's ravens, so the "ravens" supplied food for the children that day. (See 1 Kings 17) In fact, the rich man's servants had to cook the food in big utensils, not easy for the servants to carry. Yet, in spite of the difficulty of transporting so much food, the rich man's servants arrived just in time for the children's meal. The rich man and his servants tended those orphans just as they were his best friends.

It is important to God that we maintain relationship with Him, that we "abide" in Christ. The director of the orphanage, in fasting, deprived himself of food that the children might have something to eat. One can hear the words of Jesus,

> "For this reason I say to you, do not be anxious for your life, as to what you shall eat, or what you shall drink; nor for your body, as to what you shall put on. Is not life more than food, and the body than clothing? Look at the birds of the air, that they do not sow, neither do they reap, nor gather into barns, and yet your heavenly Father feeds them. Are you not worth much more than they?" (Matthew 6:25-26)

Those who live on the edge must learn to speak God's language. Fasting communicates to Him in a deep and passionate way.

LEFT FOR DEAD
K.A. PAUL OF INDIA

Chapter 11--Power In Ministry

Science tells us that for every effect there must be a cause. Nothing moves apart from a previous action—except, of course, God. The Bible teaches that nature testifies to the deeper reality of the spiritual order. (Psalm 19) If actions cause consequences in the physical, so they do in the spiritual.

What is the "engine," the driving force for power in ministry? Matthew 17 records how the disciples watched Jesus cast out a mighty demon, and were troubled they couldn't do it. Jesus tells them, in verse 21, "this kind does not go out except by prayer and fasting." Prayer with fasting is the power driving effectiveness in ministry. This is why I pray and fast for the directors, students, faculty, workers, churches, buildings and villages serving and served by Gospel to the Unreached Millions. A ministry leader must be like watchman on the walls, praying and fasting for those under his care.

CALL FOR INTERCESSION

Sometimes, a follower of Christ will sense a burden developing in his or her heart for a person, church, ministry, or situation. Such a concern should be received by the believer as a summons by the Holy Spirit to pray and fast until the burden is lifted. In fact, there is an action-reaction toward whatever you pray and fast. Pray with fasting for your enemies, and they become your friends. Pray with fasting for your family and neighbors, and you will see God touch their lives. In our ministry, we have seen whole villages turn to the Lord, as leaders prayed with fasting.

In India, we have a "dowry demon." Many young women commit suicide because their in-laws pester them for more dowry. We have learned, in the church in our nation, to bind this demon through prayer and fasting. In some remote regions of India, baby girls are even killed because the parents think they will not have a dowry for the child's wedding. In cases where the home is breaking apart because of the dowry demon, we have seen God bring healing through prayer with fasting.

In one case, we bound the demon of lusting for money, greed and ill-gotten gain. The husband received Christ. The wife had left because of the dowry pressures, but now that the husband was a "new creation in Christ Jesus," he wanted his wife back. She refused to come, fearing ill-treatment. But again, fasting with prayer broke the power of the dowry demon, and she packed her bags and came home. The couple is now living together happily and have even planted churches together. Their changed lives and marriage has had an impact on surrounding villages, where people gave recognized that Jesus changes human character.

BOUND IN STUBBORNNESS

In another situation, there was a pastor's son who was bound in stubbornness. The dad preached all over Orissa, leading hundreds to Christ, but his own boy wouldn't come to Christ. As a tot, the son plunged down a hill and was killed. The parents prayed, "Lord, if you bring him back to life, we will dedicate him for ministry." The child was miraculously restored. He grew up and became an engineer, but would have nothing to do with Christ. Several leading preachers spoke to him to no avail.

The father's heart was heavy as he traveled the State of Orissa, ministering. One day, he invited me to his home. The dad told me the story of his son, weeping. Suddenly, the young man just happened to walk in. I invited him to be seated a few minutes so I could share the Gospel with him. "Mind your own business," he said. This only deepened the father's grief.

I asked the dad to join me in an eight-day fast for the boy. We prayed for other concerns, but the young man's salvation was our primary focus. Just as we concluded the fast on the eighth day, there was a knock at my door. I was shocked to see the pastor's son standing there. What had happened? On the last day of that fast, at about midnight, we had bound the powers of darkness hindering the young man's salvation, and asked the Lord to visit him that very evening. In the wee hours before the dawning of our eighth day of fasting, the pastor's son had had a nightmare, which had propelled him to my home for counsel and comfort. I led him to Christ in my home.

A SIKH CONVERT

An even more difficult case was winning a Sikh to Christ. They are exceedingly strong in their beliefs, and follow a priest called Gurunanak. Rarely does one see a Sikh convert to Christ. However, when they do receive Christ, former Sikhs become outstanding disciples in their faith and lifestyle. Today, our Gospel to the Unreached People school has a number of former Sikhs. We also have church planters who once were Sikhs working successfully in Punjab State.

One of the mightiest evangelists in India's past was Sadhu Sunder Singh. He was truly an apostle for India. He walked the mountainous regions of Tibet, preaching the Gospel, until his feet would bleed, so was termed, "the apostle of the bleeding feet." He faced tremendous persecution. His own father wanted to kill him because Sunder Singh had accepted Christ. A key to the spiritual power in his life was fasting. Sunder Singh walked with such purity that sometimes he was mistaken for Christ Himself.

In Orissa, I was introduced to a young Sikh family. The man was robust, yet fearful. He loaded me with questions. I began to feel uneasy. He lacked peace of mind, so perhaps he was just trying to get some comfort by talking about Christ. Or, I thought, maybe he was trying to trick me. The questioning went on for days. Finally, he was convinced Christ is the Way, Truth and Life. We prayed, but fear now rose in me. I began to contemplate the possibility that if this man converted to Christ, I would be killed. Nevertheless, he joined me in prayer with fasting. During the fast, the Sikh man received Christ and said he wanted to be baptized in water.

LOSS OF MATERIAL RICHES

Sikh men identify themselves as such by wearing long beards, and signifies homage to the Sikh god. He shaved his beard for the baptism. Word spread in his area that he had become a follower of Christ. The man's wife left him. His relatives turned away, refusing to have anything to do with him. Some of them came looking for me. I had to hide, but finally came face to face with his father in law. They told me they would have nothing to do with him unless he denied Christ. The young man's reply was that he could not give up Christ "at any cost." The family tried to poison him, but failed. At last, this young former Sikh, who had received Christ during a fast, was living alone, but with Jesus. He had been incredibly wealthy, but had lost it all when driven out by family members.

I have learned much about prayer with fasting from my mother, who has been exemplary, even in long fasts. In fact, her persistence in fasting and prayer would irritate our Hindu relatives. They loved pleasure, and would watch my mother fasting and praying for lost souls. There was such an immense spiritual gulf between her and her blood kin that they simply couldn't understand what made my mother go for such long periods without food. But those who spent time with her in fasting were greatly rewarded.

Ruby was one of the blessed ones who associated with my mother in her fasting. The Bible encourages us to link to one another as we pray and so spiritual combat. There is power in agreement in prayer. (Matthew 18:19) One can put 1,000 to flight, and two 10,000. (Deuteronomy 32:30) Two are better than one to bind evil and loose people to the resources of God's Kingdom. (Ecclesiastes 4:9)

ABUSED

Sometimes when mother and Ruby would pray, they would labor long, and when Ruby arrived home, she would be beaten by her drunken husband. Though abused many times, she wouldn't give up fasting and prayer.

Mother and Ruby would weep as Jeremiah must have cried out. On one occasion, they were praying for Ruby's husband. He wanted to get rid of her, but Indian women won't leave for such reasons. Ruby had faith God would change him. She knew the meaning of "pray without ceasing." (1 Thessalonians 5:17) As she prayed, she would also be witnessing to her husband. In response, Ruby's husband even tried to kill her.

So, mother and Ruby went on a long fast for him. One night, Ruby arrived home from being with my mother very late. Her husband was ready–literally–to kill her.

"Where did you go?" he demanded.

"Sir, I have been fasting and praying for you," she answered, as gently as possible.

"I have beaten you brutally before, but today, I am going to kill you." Suddenly, his hand darted from behind, holding an ugly knife. "Before I start, call on your God!"

Ruby began praying audibly. Her husband interrupted.

"Should you fast and pray for *me*? Can your God save you from this knife in my hands? Soon it will plunge into your chest!"

Ruby continued in deep prayer, sensing the moment for her husband's deliverance was approaching. In fact, the glory of God was on her after 40 days of fasting. She felt a radiance much brighter than the gleam of the knife blade hovering over her heart. The compassion in her burned more intensely than the passionate anger in her husband.

BRILLIANT LIGHT

Just as Ruby's husband lifted the dagger to drive it into her chest, a brilliant light flashed, and knocked him to the ground. The knife thudded to the floor. Ruby's husband scrambled around, trying to understand what had happened. Then he stood. But, like Saul of Tarsus, he arose a new man. He even heard the Voice as Saul had, asking, "Why are you persecuting Me?" Ruby's spouse now went back down, flinging himself at Ruby's feet, repenting, asking her forgiveness. He received Christ immediately, and both Ruby and her husband are now full-time workers, preaching the Gospel. *Nothing is impossible for the Lord.*

Another woman, Naomi, was a widow seeking to raise six children. She bought six cows and sold the milk to provide a meager income for the family. One of her sons became seriously ill, and she rushed him to the hospital. After examining the child, Dr. Vishwanatham pronounced the boy had an incurable disease, and sent him back home with his mother to die. She pled with the doctor to help the lad. But the physician said the situation was hopeless.

Naomi carried the little boy home, her tears raining down on his body as she walked. I happened to see her along the way, and my heart melted for her. After she told me the problem, I suggested we take the child to our home instead. I told her we would call for an emergency fast.

Lazarus was four days dead and buried, and yet the Lord called him back to life," I told her. "Let's resort to the Lord of resurrection and life. After all, your son is not yet dead. We may have only a few hours, so let's fast and cry out to Him."

Then, suddenly, I had an assurance it would be well. "I am certain God will raise up your son," I told Naomi. "And he will be a testimony for Christ."

FASTING, PRAYING, CRYING

Encouraged, Naomi joined me in going to my house. Once there, we put the child on our bed. Our fellow Christians heard our urgent call, and joined us. Many were now present, fasting, praying, crying. Voices went up, and there was a God to hear. Even unsaved relatives and neighbors took an interest. Believers were learning how to seek the Lord in emergency; unbelievers were seeing that there is a Supreme Being over the affairs of individuals.

Noticeably, the boy began to improve. This only encouraged more prayer. Those fasting had no problem believing, because they had all once been idol worshippers, and God had restored them from that spiritual deadness. They knew Him as the God Who can see, hear, feel, reply and change a situation from worst to best and beyond. These stalwart warriors knew the futility of praying to an idol, but also the power in seeking the Living God.

As they prayed, the boy stirred. Then he sat on the bed. Finally, the lad the doctor has said was near death, began to walk around the room. The mother couldn'r contain her rejoicing.

There were many results. All the villagers in the region realized the power of God. The physician recognized Jesus as God. People began to respect and honor our house. It became a "healing center" for body, soul and spirit. The news was published widely. Other people brought the demonized and sick, and took them home delivered and healed. Non-Christians came, bringing their burdens, to have them lifted by Jesus. Our home came to be recognized as a place of Divine deliverance.

The home of every believer should be such a place. House churches were the pattern for the 1st century followers of Christ. One can see the pattern, even, from the Old Testament forward. The structure of Israel consisted of families, composing tribes, which, together comprised the nation. So the basic unit of the Church ought to be the home as a place of ministry. But these "house churches" ought not be separate. Just as Paul spoke of churches that met in houses, so he wrote of the "church in Rome," or Ephesus, or whatever city where Christ's people lived. So the house churches should make up congregations ("tribes") and the congregations, the whole Church, or "great congregation." But every house should be a ministry-base.

As people give their homes as centers for prayer and fasting, they will see the power of God manifest in their neighborhoods.

LEFT FOR DEAD
K.A. PAUL OF INDIA

Chapter 12--The Ministry of Healing

"Krupa" means "grace" in my native Telugu language. That is also the name of my sister, who, with her husband, Yesupadam, is a full time minister with Gospel to the Unreached Millions.

As a teenager, Krupa was attacked by a massive stroke which left her paralyzed for life. She was confined to her bed, in a constant state of suffering, wasting away. My parents had received Christ, and though greatly assaulted by the enemy, remained strong. Yet I know they shared Krupa's suffering as they watched the paralysis march through her body like a marauding army, bringing more and more of the territory of her physical life under its control. Finally, she was unable to move fingers or toes. Then she became numb and insensitive to stimuli. The left side of her body was as dead within two weeks of the stroke.

MANY SUGGESTIONS

Well-meaning neighbors and relatives had many suggestions regarding medical care. My dad had been a medical practitioner and knew how serious the situation was. Yet he could also remember how sick he had been, and how pilgrimages to temples and idols could not heal him. Yet, through prayer and fasting, Christ had healed my father totally. Since he had had a supernatural experience with God, he was convinced that Krupa should receive a Divine touch as a witness to unbelievers.

This angered his relatives and friends. They agreed my dad would be responsible for Krupa's suffering and premature death. Father was as unmovable as the mountains that surround Jerusalem. He trusted in God with such certainty that he was not stirred to fear the consequences of waiting on the Lord. He knew he had waited on the Lord three and one-half years for his healing, and he was willing to await his daughter's rescue as well.

Since God was using dad's home as a prayer center to heal many and win the lost, he felt it would be a contradiction to rush his daughter to the hospital. If he did that, the anger directed at him would have been blunted, but he felt faith in Jesus would have been quenched. Dad was also concerned that such an action would have hindered the spiritual progress of several new believers who were being taught to trust in the Great Physician for their deliverance when medical science failed.

REBUKES FOR DAD

"This madness you call faith will kill your daughter," a relative said. "Release her into our hands," another echoed, "and we will see to her welfare." With such words, they rebuked my dad severely. Even Christian friends began to advise father to get medical treatment for Krupa.

My dad was not against medical treatment. Medical science is a gift from God. All truth is by God's revelation, including that of how to cure the human body with medical skill and technology. As unbelieving Cyrus was used of God in the destiny of Israel, even unbelieving physicians can be God's instruments in healing sick people. The "how" of healing is a matter of God's sovereignty. Yet, deep inside, dad felt to release Krupa to the hospital and physicians at that point would have affected the faith of Hindu converts.

Father understood an important principle of witness: our lifestyle affects others. This is a major difference between people who know Christ and those who do not. Committed disciples of Jesus are highly sensitive to the impact they have on other people. Self-focused individuals simply do not care, as long as their personal needs are met. Every believer ought to have a concern about how his or her decisions and actions affect the whole body of Christ, as well as the watching world. For my dad, Christ was the "pearl of great price," and his priorities were centered on what would bring glory to the Lord.

My father's whole world was watching him, including people in surrounding villages. Yet there was no improvement in my sister. We all used our greatest weapon against her affliction–prayer and fasting. Relatives came to visit and saw her condition worsening. Some of them stayed, thinking we would soon have a funeral, and they didn't want to have to make the journey again.

RESOURCES FROM THE THRONE

Centuries ago, people thought the whole universe revolved around the earth. Copernicus upset that notion, by showing that the solar system revolves around the sun. The truth is, earth revolves around Heaven, which means that the resources for earthly life at its highest and best come into the earth from God's Throne, in Heaven. And that's what happened to Krupa. Even today, she does not understand nor can she explain all that happened to her.

It occurred in the middle of the night. She sensed an angel came and touched her. "Get up and walk," the heavenly being said. Then the angel told her more:

> *God has seen your fastings and heard your prayers. He knows and appreciates the steadfastness of your faith. God knows the risk your dad has taken. God admires your unwavering faith. You wanted God to get the glory fully out of your sufferings, and you wanted to extend His Kingdom through your healing.*

> *God did not put you to shame, but He has honored you.*

On the command of the angel, Krupa instantaneously arose as though she had never been paralyzed nor crippled. She walked in and out of each darkened room where her family members lay sleeping. Finally, she stood beside my parents' bed.

They stirred, and rubbed their eyes. They saw her, but thought it was a ghost or spirit. But soon, they realized that they were staring at a living, walking miracle. They looked at their daughter, who had been bed-fast for weeks, to the extent she had to have even the most intimate needs cared for by someone else. When they had gone to bed the night before, they sensed she had been in the last hours of her life. But now, here she stood, alive and well, as if she had never been stricken.

THE GREAT PHYSICIAN

An angel is but a messenger from God's Throne. My sister had actually been touched by the Great Physician. While it had seemed God had lingered, as always, He was right on time. All the watching heathen world around us saw that Jesus Christ is the same in all generations. The report of the miracle was heard by tens of thousands, and gave encouragement and hope to many suffering afflictions.

When I was being taught to ride a bicycle, my brother was pushing me on one side and my sister pulling me on the other. I crashed, and broke my right arm. This was in the period when my dad had just turned to Christ. As a fresh Hindu convert, he had been taught not to use medicine, that Christ heals without it. So, father prayed for three things: that I should have no pain, sleep soundly, and have no continuing discomfort. As a small lad, it was amazing to see dad pray that way. All three requests were granted, and my badly broken arm was healed without medical treatment. Dad put my bones in their proper places, wrapped up my arm, and prayed and fasted until I was well.

We serve a God Who heals today. He is sovereign, and He manifests healing in whom He chooses. As an evangelist, I minister in crusades where we see hundreds of thousands coming to Christ after preaching a clear and simple Gospel message for an hour or so. We then give people the opportunity to accept Christ, and then counselors follow up the converts for about a half hour, giving the new believers a five-step plan of action:

> ✓Pray to Jesus only from this forward;
> ✓Find a church to join or form a house church;
> ✓Read the Bible;
> ✓Witness to others about your experience with Christ;
> ✓Be baptized in water.

Then, at the end, I pray for the sick. Many are touched miraculously by the Lord and witness to others. We have seen entire families give their lives to Christ after experiencing the power of God.

VAST HARVEST

In fact, in early 1997, as noted in the previous chapter, we conducted a "Good News Healing Festival" at a certain city in India. Attendance the first night was 80,000. Many times, at the end of a service, I instruct those people not to return, but the next night to send their friends and neighbors. On the second night, the attendance was 150,000. It climbed to 200,000 the third night, 250,000 the fourth. On the last evening, there were more than 300,000 people present. During the entire crusade, 800,000 people prayed to receive Christ. Many had either been healed, or had seen someone at the crusade miraculously touched by the Lord, as Krupa had been.

The local crusade officers wrote:

> "We do faithfully the follow-up with the new converts of our city. But there are people who have attended from hundreds of surrounding villages. Most of them do not have Churches. So please send some of your native missionaries to these unreached villages."

This has spurred us to move quickly in raising funds for graduates of our Gospel to the Unreached Millions Bible schools to go to such villages, and plant churches.

I CAN HEAL NO ONE

In crusades, like the one described above, I pray for many needs, including physical healing. After I pray for people, I ask them to examine their bodies, and, if the healing is manifest, to thank God. I see thousands lifting up praise to Him, as they see and experience the evidence of their healing. Many also are set free from afflictions of mind and spirit. Usually, sick people are brought to my hotel for more prayer. While we see many touched instantly, some are not. They expect me to touch and heal them. But I make it clear in my preaching that I can heal no one. Their faith must be in Christ, not me. I lay them before the Father, and He is the One Who determines what will happen.

There are two extremes about the ministry of healing. One is that God no longer heals, as He did in New Testament times. The opposite is the idea that one can demand immediate healing from God, apart from His sovereignty. His promise to all His children is that He will forgive all our sins and heal all our diseases. (Psalm 103:1-3)The only issue for the child of God is when the Father will manifest the healing and how. For some, the healing may be manifest in deliverance from the stricken body, and into the wholeness of presence in Heaven.

Faith is vital in receiving healing. Many times, Jesus told people that their healing would be in proportion to their faith. He also "reckons" the faith of others to a sick person who may not have clear belief that God will heal. This was the case of the Roman Centurion, for example, whose servant was healed. See (Matthew 8) In Krupa's healing, my parents' faith was crucial. My dad stood strong on the following Scriptures:

> Exodus 15:26–"I am the Lord that healeth thee ..."
> Isaiah 53:5, 1 Peter 2:24–"By His stripes we are healed."
> Isaiah 58:8–"Thine health shall spring forth speedily."

What is faith? Many people believe it is whipping up the mind to be convinced a certain thing will happen. Even the "positive thinking" writers and teachers in the unbelieving world can endorse that. Such is not faith. As the Holy Spirit puts in Hebrews 11, faith is "substance" and "evidence." No human being can produce faith. God gives faith, and people receive it. For the unbelieving in our crusades, it is the faith of our ministry teams that God uses to pour in healing. He has given them a certainty that He will manifest health in the afflicted. For the believing individual, faith, given by God, is the "hand" into which He places the blessing of healing. But such a person does not contrive the faith. Even the faith to receive what God wants to give in healing is a gift from God!

Why does God impart such faith and consequent healing in some, but not all, every time they ask? After all, even Lazarus finally succumbed. Those healed in our crusades will someday get sick again. They may cry out to God once more, but ultimately they won't receive a manifestation of healing in this worlds. It must be remembered that Divine healing falls in the category of the miraculous. The Greek word used in the New Testament for "miracle" is *semeion*, meaning, "a sign." God sovereignly gives miracles to signify that what is preached or witnessed to is real. He affirms and testifies through miracles that the message is true. That's why signs and wonders *follow* those who believe. (Mark 16:17) The servant of God can expect to leave a trail of miracles, confirming that what he or she has declared is from God Himself!

The other side of this truth is that God doesn't give a miracle simply for a display that fulfills no purpose. This is where His sovereignty is involved. Of course, His sovereignty also means He can do a miracle anytime He wants to, whether people understand it or not.

I am not the only worker in a developing nation who is seeing such miracles. Signs and wonders are continuous works by the Holy Spirit in these nations, producing unprecedented harvest. Many in the West have heard rumors of an Acts-type ministry in frontier areas, and I can testify it is true.

LEFT FOR DEAD
K.A. PAUL OF INDIA

Chapter 13--Kidnapped In Calcutta

The banging on the door of my Calcutta hotel room that night was like a thunderclap shattering the peace of a summer afternoon.

The organized group I call in this book, Paknam, were among the fiercest opponents of the Gospel in India. They were determined to stamp me out, and had followed and harassed me many times. That night I had been thinking about the Paknam, and why they wanted me dead. At last I had come to some measure of peace. Then came the thundering knock on my door.

"You must vacate this room and move to the sixth floor," said the man at my door. He directed me to the new room. Just as I entered, I saw a number of tough-looking men. *Paknam!* As I walked in, the door behind me was slammed and locked. My eyes darted, looking for an escape. There was none. The Paknam laughed. I was trapped for certain death, they told me.

THE PLOT

They spoke to one another in their dialect.

"Do you understand what we are saying?" one of them asked me.

"I understand," I replied, grimly.

"Are you afraid?" another Paknam inquired.

"My God will protect me," I answered.

Soon, the Paknam were sleeping. But I could not doze off, nor could I think of a way of escape.

The next morning, the Paknam assaulted me with questions: Why is your God so important? How does He become unique? Why did you leave Hinduism for Christianity? How much money did you receive for becoming a Christian?

"I accepted Christ through faith and because of love," I replied. I explained that the decision to become a Christian is not for material gain. In fact, instead of receiving money, I said, we are taught to give 10 per cent of our finances to the church. Also, I told them, we Christians in India do not live the high style of Westerners. I spoke to the Paknam of how my father--a former Hindu priest--had become a follower of Jesus Christ.

The Paknam became weary of my talking. "Let's see how your God will deliver you from our hands," one of them said, glaring at me. "There will not be a single Christian living in India within five years ... they will be washed away," he smirked.

POISON

I had not eaten since arriving at the hotel. Now a man tossed food in front of me. The food was repugnant, and I didn't want to eat it. They demanded I eat. I choked down a few morsels. It appeared the food was poisoned. Violent pains soon pounded my insides. Then they tried to force me to worship idols and eat the food--called *pasadam*--offered to idols. If I ate the *pasadam*, they believed, I would be sanctified. I refused to eat or worship the idols.

I ran for the lavatory and began to drink water so I wouldn't dehydrate. The windows were shut tight so I wouldn't call for help, and the room was stuffy. The Paknam laughed at me continuously. They showed me a video about their god, and all the ceremonies and sacrifices.

"Our god wants holy blood," a Paknam told me. "You are the holy man we are going to sacrifice to our god."

"I am not holy, but a sinner saved by the Blood of Jesus," I said.

"It is a man of faithfulness we need," the Paknam said.

Then he eyed me intensely. *And that is you!*"

"I am faithful to Jesus, but not to your god," I responded.

They continued to insist I was the right person for their sacrifice.

On the third night they showed me deadly weapons. They dangled a rope in front of, telling me they would use it to tie me. Then the Paknam brought out sinister looking knives with which they would carve me. They took much pleasure in taunting me. But now a dark edge had entered their emotions: they were increasingly angry I wouldn't worship their idols.

They even tried to tempt me. "If you will change to our god, you can speak at our national convention where thousands are present," the Paknam promised. "Tell the masses that Hinduism is the oldest religion and persuade converted Christians to return to Hinduism." If I did that, I knew I would be allowed to live, perhaps even become a hero to the Paknam who wanted to kill me.

SACRIFICE SCHEDULED

"Praise our gods," they demanded, "and denounce Jesus as a liar!"

"Please, do not force me to confess something that is against my faith and conscience," I pleaded.

The Paknam discussed the situation among themselves. "This man will not change in spite of persecutions, so let us sacrifice him to our gods in the early hours of the morning," I heard them say.

This left me numb and distressed. I could hardly speak. I refused my last meal. Nor could I sleep. Desperately I wanted to speak to my wife on the telephone. I wanted to tell her that I had to die because I wouldn't give up my faith in Jesus Christ. The Paknam would not allow me to call her.

My thoughts trailed back to the previous morning, April

6, when I had left her and my children to journey to Calcutta.

As I awoke on April 6, 1990, I did not know the harrowing experience that awaited me in Calcutta. The day's responsibilities flooded my thoughts as I arose. I began to pray. I went through the prayer list: a planned crusade in Calcutta; making application for a visa to travel to the United States, where I was to preach in Houston, Texas; polishing my English so I could preach there without an interpreter.

After an hour of prayer, I helped myself to a cup of tea. Mary and I by now had been blessed with a daughter who we named Grace. We breakfasted together as a family. It was a pleasant time. Then I walked to the train station, and boarded the train bound for Calcutta.

Now I was alone, traveling to Calcutta, the huge port city on the north side of the Bay of Bengal. It is a steamy city crammed with millions of people, 99 percent of whom are heathen. Calcutta's teeming masses are among the unreached millions to whom God has called me. I looked forward to preaching the Gospel there in a crusade.

DANGEROUS GROUPS

There are groups there intensely opposed to the Gospel of Jesus Christ. Their opposition is not limited to arguments, and they are dangerous, threatening physical harm to those who preach Christ. Like Saul of Tarsus, they consider it a high calling and duty to snuff out the message of Christ and His Kingdom. They do not want the Name of Christ even mentioned in India, and have cruelly killed numbers of Christian workers. Among these fanatics is a group dedicated to executing missionaries and new converts, the Paknam.

Throughout the train ride, I noticed eight different men staring at me constantly. I imagined they were planning something against me. When I glanced at them, they quickly diverted their eyes. I sensed they were following me to Calcutta, and prayed they were not Paknam.

Arriving in Calcutta, they followed me to the American Embassy, where I applied for my visa to visit the United States. It took a long time, filling out papers and waiting for the business to be concluded. When I came outside the Embassy, the stalkers were still there, waiting. They tailed me as I started to my hotel. Now I knew they were Paknam. I tried to outsmart them, but I couldn't shake the glowering men. I jumped into a cab, but they followed. Suddenly I bolted from the cab and dove into a crowd. Under cover of the mob, I drifted to me hotel. The Paknam were not there. I went into my room and fell to my knees thanking God for delivering me.

WHY SUCH HATE?

I reflected on why the Paknam were after me. They hate the preaching the Gospel, and malice flows from them like lava from a seething volcano. They hate to see people turn to Christ. They knew our ministry was winning multitudes. As people grasped the fact that Jesus is the only answer to their misery, they would turn to Him in huge numbers. Plus, God was delivering people from all kinds of situations. Gang members, prostitutes, zealous Hindus, professional people, rich and poor, were accepting Jesus as the only Savior and Lord. Even some who themselves had been worshipped as "gods" turned to the living Christ.

My mind turned to Gadag, one of those who had been revered as a deity. He enjoyed playing the part of the "god." Long black hair flowed down his back and a forest of beard dangled down on his saffron robe. A special mark on his forehead signalled that Gadag was a sorcerer with extraordinary evil power. He was doing things beyond human ability.

Once, I was gathered with some believers, worshipping God. Suddenly Gadag rushed on me, waving his evil magic rod around me, and calling out to his demonic powers. I stood before him, and prayed, aloud: "Jesus, may Your authority by known on earth as it is in Heaven!"

Gadag shouted back, "be speechless by the power of many gods!"

The Spirit of the living God was with me. I prayed and looked right into his eyeballs without the least movement. I laughed as I said, "you will not be able to move your hand."

Immediately, Gadag became speechless and motionless. He couldn't stir his hand! The very hand he had stretched before me now became limp. Then I prayed for him 20 minutes before he could speak or move the hand. His evil power could not withstand Christ's righteous authority. We both fell to our knees, and I led Gadag in praying to receive Christ. He was totally saved and delivered. The congregation exploded in joy.

IMMENSE CHALLENGE

The Paknam may have also wanted me dead because of another man, named Predar. In 1986, an acquaintance, Pooha, came to me with a challenge regarding Predar, a well-known magician in his village. "If you can turn Predar to Christ, I will give you 10,000-rupees." Such an amount was an average year's salary for many in India.

The challenge was immense, because many believe Christ can save just about everyone but the magicians. They are totally in the hands of Satan, living and moving by satanic power. The take an oath to serve the leader of the demons, named "kali"-- whose name is at the root of *Cal*cutta. If a servant of kali withdraws from the oath, the demons will destroy him and his family. So, with the help of evil powers, such magicians are able to perform mighty tricks and deeds. Just as a Christian gives himself or herself to Jesus, such magicians yield themselves to the tools of the devil himself. It's not surprising, then, that many believe the magicians like Predar are beyond salvation.

Predar was a tall, swarthy man who seemed wrapped in shadow. He was rebellious against any authority, since he considered himself a "god." He used his powers to perform tricks that attracted crowds, and made himself famous in his region. The ungodly chase after vain, empty, futile things, and Predar played to such audiences. He also used his wife, who was beautiful, to draw the mobs.

He would place an ordinary brick in the midst of the audience, and chant prayers. Then, he would challenge the people to move the brick. Many attempted, but none could succeed. The brick was immoveable, and the people would begin acclaiming Predar a "god," and start worshipping him.

YEAR-LONG PRAYER

I prayed for Predar an entire year, and witnessed to him about the power of Jesus. But he wouldn't give attention. I begged the Lord to change him. But God will not take away a person's free will, and so nothing happened. Then I resorted to fasting as I prayed for Predar.

At the end of one three-day fast, I went to his house and knocked on the door. A spirit of authority was on me, and, with boldness and confidence, I said, "I need to talk to you!" As I entered Predar's home, I saw idols and occultic art-works everywhere. But I spoke about the power of Jesus Christ. I looked at Predar, and told him Jesus was so powerful He could change Predar. I told him about the grace of Jesus, and now Predar became attentive. He was composed, and I could tell the Holy Spirit was working in his heart.

I kept giving Predar the Good News. Now he began to weep. Predar began to see that he was not a "god," but a mortal man, destined to die without the real God if he didn't receive Jesus' Life. At the very mention of the Name of Jesus, Predar confronted his own powerlessness and emptiness. He had to admit that his magic didn't satisfy his deepest spiritual yearnings. It was merely a profession to him, a way to make money. All the excitement of the tricks, the demons, the crowds gave him no inner satisfaction. Though he projected a formidable outward appearance, the truth was he was empty and inside and felt the stinging pain in his heart. Man is satisfied only when the living God occupies the temple of a person's body. This is the highest and best purpose for a human being. The superficial is only for a season. For Predar, that season had passed.

PREDAR SET FREE

Predar was ready, so I began to pray for him. I spoke first to God for Predar's salvation. Then, through Jesus' Name, I rebuked, bound and cast out the evil powers to which Predar was enslaved. I watched as he was set loose from the grip of darkness. Now he himself prayed, confessing he was a sinner and his need for Christ, and His salvation of grace. Suddenly, Predar declared, "this is great and wonderful!" He shouted his joy, and, in his new liberation, began to worship God.

In fact, not long afterward, Predar began sharing his testimony with others. Many wondered about his experience, and some believed. Others jeered at him, finding it hard to believe such a man would give his life to Christ. Now the man the multitude had once called "god" was telling them Jesus is the only true God.

It was amazing for Predar to be converted to Christ, humanly impossible. I was grateful to Pooha and his challenge, else Bagh might never have been reached, or been on my prayer and fasting list. As for Pooha, he really hadn't expected Predar would be saved, and so I had to release him from the promise of

$10,000-rupees.

It was the conversion of highly visible people and faithful, known servants of the evil one that had gotten the attention of the Paknam, who had followed me to Calcutta, and were now stalking me. Back in my hotel room, shuddering and praying, thanking God for my escape, I could not help but think danger from their hands was a small price to pay for leading people like Bagh to Christ.

It was at that very moment the loud knock came to my door, leading to the kidnapping I described above.

After my miraculous escape and a time for rest in my home town, I knew I had to return to the mission. My parents and wife were concerned for my safety, as I was for that of my whole family. Encouraged by my pastor, I set out once more, accompanied my some of my relatives who traveled with me part of the way. One cannot be a secret servant of God. We minister in the open. Because the Paknam have branches all over India, our openness made us an easy target. They were furious that I been delivered from them in Calcutta.

STALKED

So, another Paknam group began to stalk me on the train once more. I battled fear, and thanked the Lord there were godly men around me on the train. Their presence and prayers eased my tensions. In fact, we were able to sit together, and not be scattered throughout the train. It took 15 hours to travel 240 miles. Every 15 to 30 minutes, the train would stop for a long time. At one point, the train halted for a full hour. We could hear angry shouting. "Open the door! Bring him out!" As the fanatics drew near, I became fearful. I prayed earnestly. My relatives imparted courage to me. But I knew I had to get strength from above.

To elude the Paknam, we decided to travel another route,

and head back home. After an hour of journeying, we left the train. But the Paknam caught on, and followed. One of them edged up to me, and snarled, "today is your last ... you cannot escape." The whole Paknam grouped seethed at us. But be tried to pay them no attention.

We hopped a bus, and they were on right behind us. In the middle of the jungle, they told the driver to stop the bus. They had determined among themselves this was the place to sacrifice me to the god of jungles. The driver refused, and we reached home. I saw my wife and child. Several friends and co-workers were there as well, along with my in-laws. They didn't know I was still in trouble. But now I knew we had arrived safe at home one more time by the grace of God.

'WE WILL KILL YOU'

Later, the telephone rang. It was a threat from the Paknam. At 2 a.m., there was another call. "We will kill you within a month if you do not leave this place," said the voice. My wife and I were distressed. Our friends were guarding us, and had also informed the police, who were not so helpful. Our loved ones did guard duty night after night. Even in the daylight hours, some performed sentry duty at our house. We spent 26 days in this plight, fasting and praying. I was so proud of Mary, who held up courageously. I thanked God daily for His moment by moment provision of grace and protection. He reminded us, as He did Joshua, "I will not fail thee, nor forsake thee."

One day, a Paknam man phoned, and my wife got the call. I was standing nearby, and could tell by her expression what was happening. Suddenly, I was flooded with power and authority by the Holy Spirit. I grabbed the phone.

"I will neither leave this city nor quit the ministry!" I told him. "We will serve God for our whole lifetime no matter what happens."

Then, I had a flash of inspiration, and spoke it to the anonymous caller. I named a certain time, and said, "I am coming to the public square in the center of the city, and I will walk among you."

Early the morning I was to walk among the Paknam, I went all over the town, telling people that if I lived, I would continue to serve God. For me, life and ministry cannot be disconnected. I am ready to die in ministry, but if I live, I will live for God and His ministry. That determination gave me a new liberty. Tears and worry took wings. I told people as I went through the town, "if I am alive I will serve God; if not, I will die and be with Jesus." People were shocked. But I was tired of living with fear. I discovered that day that we need not fear man nor spiritual enemies. We simply commit ourselves to God and His ministry--no matter what. And that day, I called the bluff of the Paknam. As Jesus walked through the threatening crowds at Nazareth, so I made my way through the mobs in the public place that day.

HACKED TO PIECES

Gradually, many in India are realizing that persecuting Christians is wrong. We now live amicably among Hindus and others, with respect. Those who knew me discovered they could not change nor stop me with threats and beatings so severe at times they left me for dead. But there are still tragedies. In 1994, as I noted earlier, my beloved co-laborer Paul James was hacked into six pieces by extremists. He felt his calling to be that of planting churches in dangerous places, so he would not stop, despite threats and warnings. He left behind three children. His wife always supported his zeal for ministry, and still works with the ministries he left behind.

A major objective of Gospel to the Unreached Millions (GUM), our ministry organization, is to help support native missionaries. Our goal is to train at least one million national workers to reach all the unreached villages of the 62 countries within the "10-40 Window," the region of the world least evangelized. We have a blue print, a clear strategy for penetrating these seemingly impenetrable places. Yet the body of Christ is too exhausted from infighting to vigorously forge ahead. There is an urgent need in the church to come to agreement on foundational doctrine, and not waste time debating and fighting over the non-essentials.

Once, I was questioned by religious authorities about the style by which I baptize people in water. They wanted to know: Do I baptize backwards or forwards? This illustrates how we lose focus on the main objective of evangelism. In some countries, people are dipped into the water three times—once in the Name of the Father, again in the Name of the Son, and the third time, in the Name of the Holy Spirit. Some might immerse forwards, some backwards, some ever sideways. The only way I could never devise to baptize was upside down!

CONSUMING FELLOWSHIP

But why are such useless debates consuming fellowship among believers? While it is true that obedience in water baptism is crucial for opening up the person to a deeper walk with the Lord, it is the Blood of Jesus that saves and cleanses. We major in the minors and lose the major battles with the enemy. It is time for the body of Christ to repent of her waste of God's treasures and join hands and hearts to destroy the works of the devil and see the battle pressed to its ultimate victory.

The enemy has deceived us and isolated us from one another. If we disagree on some points, let's acknowledge our disagreement, but unite in goal and strategy of finishing the task Jesus laid out for us 2,000 years ago to make disciples in all the nations. The task that could have been done in a century has taken us 2,000 years, and still a huge portion of the world's population has yet to hear even the Name of Christ.

In the West, it is often assumed that we need complicated and costly tools for this mission. Actually, the needs are simple and basic. For example, God has used Gospel for the Unreached Millions to supply hundreds of bicycles for these itinerant servants of God. The bikes are much more important to these simple warriors than costly computers. The indigenous missionaries with whom we work have planted more than 1,000 churches at this writing, and see many people come forward to accept Christ in crusades. GUM operates several training centers in the 10-40 Window area, which train and equip leaders for churches to be planted among unreached people.

'KNEEOLOGICAL' PREPARATION

More than 90 per cent of our students come for our basic training, and some stay for a full nine months. While theological training is important, we also want them to spend many hours in "kneeological" preparation. Holy Spirit-led training is the most important for the immense challenges these students face when they leave our schools. Some of them--like me--will be beaten and left for dead.

The devil and his demons are not omniscient. Many times, they have looked with glee on servants of God lying in a pool of blood, from a beating, or a stoning, or a hacking. They've watched as people caught in the bondage of their violence have turned and left us for dead. But the destroyer and his forces have been disappointed again and again, as God's people, left for dead, have risen from the dust, only to advance the Kingdom with more determination and boldness than ever.

The devil simply doesn't understand that everytime he leaves one of us for dead, a garden of life is planted.

At 3 a.m. I had one hour before I was to be sacrificed. I went to the toilet, and there I prayed intensely. I spoke to God about how He had delivered Shadrach, Meshach and Abednego from the fiery furnace and Daniel from the lion's den. I kept repeating Scriptures to myself. God was my only comfort. Somehow, I knew He was with me. I even asked Him to take me away bodily as He did Enoch and Elijah. "Do not let these people kill me," I prayed. "It would be better for You to kill me!" I yearned to see my family, and for them to pray for me.

THE VOICE OF PEACE

Suddenly, peace washed over my heart. Talking to the living God made all the difference. I heard a sweet Voice deep inside my heart:

> *"I am the God of Abraham, Isaac and Jacob. I am God, the Deliverer and Redeemer, Who redeemed Israel from the bondage of Egypt and Pharaoh. I AM WITH YOU. Fear not, My son. I love you. I have neither left you nor forsaken you."*

My heart rejoiced at the sound of my Father's Voice. I felt life returning to me. I soared into a spirit of praise and worship.

Suddenly, I heard another Voice deep down in my heart. "Walk away now ... leave this place." I glanced around. The doors were closed and locked. Again, the Voice: *Walk away now!"*

As I walked out of the bathroom, all the Paknam were fast asleep. The loud snores covered my footsteps. In fact, the men were like dead animals. All I wore was my scanty night dress. Nevertheless, I walked slowly to the door which I knew to be locked. Yet it was open! I was certain the angel of the Lord had opened the door.

The elevator was not working, so I went down the steps.

"What are you doing? It's only 3:30 in the morning," someone asked.

I gasped. Miraculously, the man I encountered was an old friend. How he happened to be in that precise place at 3:30 in the morning could only have been a work of God. The literal meaning of "angel" is "messenger." He was like an angel, because he was the messenger of God to me that night. In a city of millions, the one person I met in my escape was my friend! I explained my plight. He brought me shoes and clothes and escorted me to a friend of his who was a government official, who escorted us to the airport. I kept looking over my shoulder, concerned that the Paknam would be following. Finally, my "angel" friend and I boarded the airplane for my home city of Visakhapatnam, which is south of Calcutta, on the Bay of Bengal. Thankfully, the Paknam were not on the plane. My friend traveled with me all the way to Visakhapatnam.

MY 'ANGEL'

There, we went to a hotel, where Matthew joined us. This was the man who baptized me. Though he was now an old man physically, he was young in spirit, still planting churches. To be with Matthew after my harrowing experience in Calcutta was heavenly. We sat and I told my friends what happened. Afterward, I slept soundly. My "angel" friend returned to Calcutta later that morning, and went to the hotel where I had been held captive. The Paknam had left, and he searched for my belongings, finding everything but my watch.

Meanwhile, Pastor Matthew drove me to my parents' home. I reported to them my kidnapping in Calcutta. I decided not to return to Calcutta nor to Orissa State, where we knew my life to be in danger. A few days later I awoke realizing I had to go back to Orissa, where my wife and Grace were. Plans were made to get them out, but I determined to go myself. So, with my brother-in-law and friends, we travelled back there by train.

I knew danger could not keep me from telling my beloved countrymen the good news of Jesus Christ. In fact, I had been in many dangerous places before, tortured, beaten and left for dead. But God had once given me a stark vision of the unreached millions perishing in hell. I thanked God for rescuing me from my captors, and for providing my "angel" friend and the government official at exactly the right moment, and rededicated myself to telling others about the One Who can save people from hell.

God's Word says He "knows the days of the blameless; and their inheritance will be forever." (Psalm 37:18) As I told the Paknam, I have no righteousness in my own flesh, but I am cleansed by the Blood of Jesus. That makes me "blameless," through Christ. So, I believe the "number" of my days--and for all people made blameless by Jesus--is known to my Father. No person can take away the life of God's submitted servant until the "number" of those days, and the mission assigned to him or her, has been reached.

The story from Palli, Orissa State, with which I opened this book, reveals that as clearly as any experience I have ever had.

LEFT FOR DEAD
K.A. PAUL OF INDIA

Chapter 14--Back To Life

For many days, after the fearsome night spent in the house in Palli--described in the first chapter--I did not return to the village. But the faces of those faithful new believers who had risked their lives from me were always before me. I was their pastor. There was so much more I needed to teach them. I couldn't abandon them. My friend Abraham and I got on our bikes and peddled back.

Before we could enter the village, we were spotted. The man who saw us yelled for others to join him. But before they could catch us, we zoomed out of the village, escaping by peddling fast. Once again we were safe, but I couldn't forget the new Christians in Palli. I prayed for them night and day, asking that the Holy Spirit guide and protect them.

A friend invited me back to Palli for a visit. At night, I was able to slip into the village unseen. So I thought. My friend left me sitting in his little house, which had no electricity, while he ran out on an errand. My heart fluttered with discomfort.

ANGRY VOICES

Meanwhile, my host's mother, a boy and an elderly woman asked me questions about Jesus, salvation, and other spiritual matters. But I was increasingly uneasy. After 10 minutes, someone closed and locked the outside door. Angry voices pierced the room from outside, where I could see a crowd forming. There was no time to wait. Like an American football player, I charged the tin door, crashing through it with my shoulder. Once out, I dashed away from the mob, and made it to a neighbor's house, where I was sheltered. One more time, I had escaped my enemies in Palli.

There were other close calls there, but I knew I had to return. Psalm 144:1 says,

> Blessed be the LORD, my rock, who trains my hands for war, and my fingers for battle ...

So, in the spirit of that passage, I was spending as much as five hours a day praying for the situation in Palli. This was spiritual war. There were humans involved, but the real enemy was the devil and his demons. My only weapon and guide was prayer and faith in Christ. I asked God, "What is next?"

Most of the Palli believers could meet with us in a church I had planted in a village nearby. There was an advantage in having two churches meet together. Unity was strengthened, and it saved my travel time. Yet some of the Christians from Palli were unable to come. We discussed the need to return to Palli. Some felt strongly we should not travel there, while others implored us to come. I and my companions probed the Scriptures. What would Jesus and His apostles do?

SHAKE OFF THE DUST

For a brief time, Matthew 10:14 sounded good to me. There, Jesus had told His disciples that when a village rejected them and the Gospel, they were to shake the dust from their feet and go to another village. We decided not to go back to Palli.

Yet, inside, the Holy Spirit had not released me from that little town. In fact,m rising up within me was the sense that God wanted to a great work in Palli. Other Scriptural examples flooded my mind. Persecution always bring great results. That was the message I got as I contemplated the stories of people like Shadrach, Meschach and Abednego. Daniel had been thrown into the lion's den. Paul had been beaten, shipwrecked, and left for dead. God's message had advanced greatly with every torment suffered by His people.

Little did I know that a fate like the Apostle Paul's awaited me.

I realized it would be Biblically sound to shake the dust from me feet, and never return to Palli, as well as to go back there. Yet when I tried to fix in my mind I would not return, there was no peace. Finally, I prayed to God, "I will do whatever You want." It was at that point I got clear direction.
 I read about the faith of Moses:

> By faith Moses, when he had grown up, refused to be called the son of Pharaoh's daughter; choosing rather to endure ill-treatment with the people of God, than to enjoy the passing pleasures of sin; considering the reproach of Christ greater riches than the treasures of Egypt; for he was looking to the reward. (Hebrews 11:24-26)

In the light of my struggles about going to Palli, this passage took on new freshness. Moses, I realize, had chosen to suffer with God's people rather than a life without persecution.

It was becoming clearer and clearer. I was an unmarried man, young, energetic. God was preparing me for challenges ahead. He had shown me that He will use persecutions to advance His Kingdom. If I went to Palli, I shouldn't expect *not* to be persecuted. That would be part of the mission!

At a Sunday service, I preached about Shadrach, Meshach and Abednego. As I recounted the story of these Jewish boys hurled into a furnace for God's Name, I real;realized how the miracle of their deliverance exalted God in the eyes of unbelievers. As the words flowed from my mouth, I was hearing something else inside: *I am not to fear men, but continue to minister in Palli.*

After the service, a young man seemed to confirm that. "We should not fear," he told me. "Let's go back to Palli."

We all prayed. It was decided to go back the next day for a Monday night Bible study. The little congregation escorted me into the village. Two young men went ahead as scouts. We arrived around seven that night. Several others joined us for the study. After praying, we sang, with great joy:

> *I am glad that Jesus lifted me,*
> *Singing, glory, hallelujah,*
> *Jesus lifted me.*

About 10, we concluded the meeting. In God's Presence there was no fear, and we started from the house unafraid. As we walked toward the edge of town, we could see a faint glow ahead. As we neared, we could see it was a kerosene lamp. A mob of at least 60 men clustered around it. They closed on us, and I found myself face to face with Vic, the gang leader.

"Why are you back again?"

I had no response.

Vic turned to his crowd. "Why are you just standing here watching?" With that, the mob started battering me.

A faithful member of our congregation stood between me and the crowd. "Please," he begged, "do not beat this innocent young man. He harmed no one. We invited him and he came. Beat me and kill me before you do anything to him!"

Vic's mob shoved him aside. Several other members of the congregation tried to intervene, but all were roughed up and tossed aside—even the women.

The blows now fell on me like a storm of hammers. I clutched the Bible that was so dear to me. I knew none of my human friends could help me now. I decided to run, darting along a path at the back of the town. I spotted a five-foot wall and leapt over it. But I dropped my Bible. I scampered to the house of a friend, who was studying. He had been converted through one of our meetings. I explained the situation. He locked me inside his house and went to hide in a nearby tree. No one knew where I was except that young man. He even put the lock on the outside of the door, to give the impression no one was inside.

The mob turned the village inside out looking for me. They went back to the house where we had had the prayer meeting. Congregation members thought I was hiding inside, and tried to block the door. Again, they were hurled aside. The crowd's anger intensified when they didn't find me in the house.

CROUCHING, TREMBLING

At my friend's hut, I was crouched under a small cot. My badly beaten body trembled violently. I prayed simply, "God, protect me." It was then I thought my parents and others I loved so much. "Lord," I whispered, "please let me not die this soon. There is so much I want to do. Lord, spare my life."

Just then another thought blitzed my mind. I heard Jesus, praying in Gethsemane, "Father, if it be possible, let this cup pass from Me ... but Father, not My will, but yours be done." (Matthew 26:39)

As I prayed these last words, I heard voices outside. "He's in there!" I almost died when I heard the shout, just outside the window. "I'm finished," I muttered to myself.

Meanwhile, the young owner of the hut crawled out of the tree, and nonchalantly walked up to the door of his house. "Why are you all shouting at my house?" he asked.

"Is he inside?" one of the mob asked, nose to nose with my friend.

"Is who inside?"

"We found his Bible by the fence. He's your friend."

Then the men pushed the young man aside.

"He's hiding Paul inside," another shouted. "Break down the door!"

Inside, I was certain I was moments from death.

The door was smashed open. Vic ran in, followed by six burly, angry men. They smashed the cot, and jerked me to the middle of the room. There they beat me until they dragged me to the ditch where they left me for dead.

MANY WITNESSES

Many people witnessed these events. They tell me that though I was unconscious, I was still speaking. I can take no credit, because in their language, I called out, as Stephen did, echoing his Lord, "Jesus, forgive them ... They don't know what they're doing." (Acts 7:59)

After the mob broke up, neighbors came and poured water over my face. I was barely alive. They struggled to keep me breathing. Members of our congregation in Palli came to help. The police had been informed, and arrived on the scene quickly. They took me into protective custody. In fact, most of the gang had been arrested and taken to police headquarters the same night.

It was about midnight when I regained consciousness. Police officers began dousing me with questions. I couldn't marshall my thoughts. Words were garbled as I tried to utter them. The police showed me the men who were arrested, asking over and over again, "Do you recognize this one?"

My clearing mind did begin to recognize the people in the photographs. But I would not identify them to the police. The sweet Voice of the Holy Spirit kept saying within, "Forgive them ... they know what they have done ... Christ has forgive you, and you forgive them."

With a faint, almost inaudible voice, I spoke the words tat

were in my heart. "I forgive them, and Christ loves them." Tears welled up in the eyes of the senior police officer.

'CRAZY ANIMALS'

The case officer was a young Muslim who knew me well. I had witnessed to him about Christ several times, and he loved and respected me for preaching the Gospel. "Reverend Paul, do not tie my hands. These guys must be punished severely. They have done such terrible things. They almost killed you, and for no reason. They should not be forgiven. These are crazy animals. You were damaged badly, and may not survive. Even if you do, these people will kill you completely. We know them."

He paused for a breath, and gazed at me. His caring eyes searched mine. I could tell he was wondering how I could forgive my assailants. "Please, let me take charge of them and send them off to jail."

The senior officer, watching all this, said, "Here is a true Christian ... and I want to follow Christ from today. He received Christ into his heart that very day.

Though I forgave the persecutors, they still had to face trial. There were other witnesses. When I was called to testify, I had opportunity to speak again about the true God and forgiveness. The magistrate and other officials were all astonished, and talked among themselves. "Here is a Christian," they said.

I praise God. It was His work. He did what He said He would. He performed a mighty work in Palli. And through His healing power, in several months I healed from the assault.

Ten days after my beating, some gang members were riding in a small vehicle. One, seated in the middle of the front seat, began boasting about my beating. "The young preacher will not survive," he swore. "And even if he does, he will be killed in less than 30 days." A few minutes later, the vehicle went out of control and struck an onrushing truck. The young man who was boasting of my death was killed on the spot. His companions were all safe and sound.

The news of this spread quickly, and the fear of God came on many people. Vic, the gang leader, came to me with others of his group, as I was recovering. They fell at my feet and wept. They repented to God, and asked me, "please, pray and ask God to forgive us."

HEAVEN TOUCHED EARTH

"He will forgive you," I responded. Then I led them in prayer and prayed for them. It seemed a piece of Heaven touched earth. My pains seemed to vanish as I saw these young men weeping and repenting.

Later, our whole congregation was filled with joy. Vic shared with us. "I could not sleep peacefully for eight nights. I have had dreams and painful visions. I was looking for this Paul," he said. He stopped to pray, then looked at me. "I am so very sorry for what I have done to you. But here onwards, we will be friends forever."

Not only did Vic become my faithful friend, but, as I write, he is associate pastor of the church at Palli! Sometimes this former gang leader testifies in front of thousands in our crusades. He shares what Christ has done for him. He quips, "If any of you are trying to beat this man and persecute him, you will be his next friend and fellow worker in Christ ... Blessed be the Name of the Lord!"

Another of the gang members that night in Palli beat me more ferociously than any one else. But he is also now a powerful preacher and full time pastor. Yet another of the men serves as driver of our ministry van, and carries us all around so that others can know of Christ.

This, then, is my story. Why have I told it? Not to focus attention on myself. But I have shared the account of my life and testimony in Christ because it is illustrative of what scores of believers walk through daily.

The Western world has little direct knowledge of what is required for people to be faithful to Christ in nations where people are largely unreached. As individuals see the determined commitment of those who are persecuted for Christ, they wonder at the awesomeness of the Lord Who elicits such faithfulness. The endurance of Christ's people under immense persecution is a witness to the beauty and truth of Jesus.

THE STORY OF MANY

In this book, I have told of my life. But it's also the story of Paul James and many other native missionaries who are nameless and faceless to the church outside the 10-40 Window. Many live in such obscurity that they are hardly known within their own region. I dedicate this volume to those brave servants of God who face hardship and death from every direction. These native missionaries face wild beasts, pestilences, thieves, harsh climate, rough paths, deep jungles, meager finances, lack of medical care and sanitary conditions, miles of travel by foot, no schools for their children, seldom a permanent home, bad water, hostile people. Yet none of this stops them. They sleep on the ground, minister out in the open, eat simply.

And they are not just in India. I think of believers crucified in the late 20th century in Sudan. There are stalwart followers of Jesus who live under constant threat in rabid Muslim countries. The 20th century has been a period of martyrdom for many of Christ's people under ruthless communist tyrants, as well as fascist dictators.

The story of K.A. Paul is the epic of such indigenous servants of God throughout the developing nations, some of whom, like me and the New Testament apostle for whom I'm named, have been left for dead and come back with more energy, zeal and passion than ever before.

GOSPEL TO THE
Unreached Millions
PO Box 60703
Houston TX 77205
281-548-1040